ADRIATICO

RECIPES AND STORIES FROM
ITALY'S ADRIATIC COAST

PAOLA BACCHIA

Smith
Street
Books

CONTENTS

INTRODUCTION

My father grew up on the shores of the Adriatic Sea.

I have a photo of him from that time; he is floating in the shallow waters of the Adriatic, looking straight at the camera. He's young, strong and full of belief in his place in that world. But it was the summer of 1940 and the world was changing at a rate beyond anyone's control and he, like millions of others, would hurtle through those years to whatever fate the hard miracle of survival presented to them.

My father's fate was to lose his home and his birthright, and so he became one more member of the Italian diaspora who had to board a ship with a single suitcase in hand and watch their homeland dissolve into the horizon as the ship sailed from port.

Years later, in the quiet of our home in suburban Melbourne, Australia, he told me that before the war his mother (my nonna Stefania) would wrap freshly fried sardines or mackerel in paper and carry them down to the beach. Together with his father and sister, they would sit on the rocks and eat the fish, still warm from the kitchen and so fresh it still tasted of the sea.

The shores were swathed with rocks and shallow rock pools, and the sea from where the fish had been caught the night before was limpid and blue. He held onto these memories for the rest of his life: the clear waters, being with his family, the long summer with its slanted evening light picking its way across the sea before it vanished beyond the Italian peninsula, and the fish from the sea's northernmost waters: sardines, cuttlefish and bream.

The Italian coast of the Adriatic Sea runs from the heel of the boot-shaped peninsula at the Ionian Sea to the northern waters of the Gulf of Trieste, before it loops around to Slovenia and Croatia. State route SS16 is called the Adriatica and it skirts much of the coast. If you follow it northwards from its most southern point, where groves of olive trees twist their roots into the undulating red earth, you will see a changing landscape.

Along the way, spindly fishing machines reach out into the sea from the coast of the 'trabocchi'; at the Conero mountain, trees bend at impossible angles to almost touch the water; and when you reach the mouth of the Po River, you will discover wetlands that are home

to hundreds of varieties of birds. White-washed walled 'masserie', colourful villages and sea-facing piazze dot the 1200 kilometre (745 mile) coastline, with the sea being a strong connector of those living on its shores.

Standing on the coast down near the pointed end of Italy's heel, at the white-walled town of Otranto, if you look over the water on a clear day you might just see Albania on the opposite shore. It's not that far by boat if you sail with the wind, and in the days before cars and well-made roads, sea travel was far easier than land travel. According to Sandro, a native of the town of Poggio in Le Marche, people in towns and villages along the upper and central Adriatic coast felt more connected to their neighbours across the sea in Dalmatia and Istria (now Croatia) than to their inland Italian cousins. Sandro shared the stories handed down to him of the Dalmatians who fled across the sea to Le Marche to escape the invading Turks.

The Dalmatians helped build Sandro's home town of Poggio and became part of the community. Their heavy imprint remains in the fabric of many towns, such as Ravenna and Venice where you will see 'pietra d'Istria', a dense white limestone from Istria, hauled over the sea to make many buildings. Trade and transport over the sea were common. For instance, olive oil from the Salento (on Italy's east coast) was loaded onto ships that sailed to Naples (on Italy's west coast) because it was easier to risk the pirates of the Mediterranean than trying to drive on the poorly made cross-country roads.

Legend has it that the Grotta degli Schiavi, in the Conero, was where Balkan pirates would hide prisoners, tying them to metal rings that still exist in the now-inaccessible seaside cave. Piracy was rife in the Adriatic until the early 1800s. Watch-towers were built along the Italian coast to warn of approaching ships and to guard from attack. The southernmost part of Puglia, a narrow finger of land that points into the Mediterranean, was repeatedly invaded; and each time the invading population would leave traces in the names of towns, the architecture, the agriculture, the language and, of course, in the food that the Pugliesi continue to make and eat every day.

This is true for the whole of the Italian Adriatic coast: the food eaten by the people who live on or near its shores is a cypher for the memories and traditions of peoples past and present. The differences found along the coast are partly due to the presence of the invaders – a 500-year-old Austrian legacy is revived daily in the kitchens of Italians who live in the Gulf of Trieste, and a spectacularly ancient Greek legacy inhabits the food of the Salento. They owe their culture of olives at least in part to the Greeks.

The ingredients used in different areas along the coast echo what was readily available, which is influenced by the climate and terrain. You won't find broad (fava) beans on many menus north of the Po River, but you will find them all over the south, especially in Puglia. I haven't found many places that use dried sweet chilli peppers in the kitchen except on the coast of the trabocchi, where they are used as the base of many dishes.

There are places along the Adriatic coast where the mountains touch the sea, resulting in a happy marriage of ingredients that are not commonly associated with each other: mushrooms and clams, silverbeet and squid, and potatoes and mussels. In the south dishes are primarily vegetarian (except for feast days), perhaps flavoured with salted anchovies, and pasta is mostly made without eggs – a comparative luxury in the spare conditions of Italy's south. However, in the north we find a greater use of meat and eggs, and pasta is typically made with eggs.

While there are many differences along the length of the coast, there are many similarities, too. The Adriatic is a wedge of the Mediterranean Sea and the catch of fish and seafood is consistent along its shores; sardines, anchovies, squid, shrimps, mussels and sole can be found in most fishing ports, from north to south. You are likely to find fish stew (brodetto) on menus all along the coast, with notable differences in ingredients, cooking methods and accompaniments. A brodetto from Porta Recanati in Le Marche is made with saffron and white wine, with not a tomato in sight; in Chioggia on the Venetian Lagoon, butter is used in the base alongside olive oil, and you will probably be offered a side of polenta; and in Vasto, on the coast of the trabocchi in the south, the fish will be laced with chilli and basil, and you will be served crusty bread to mop up the fiery red pan juices.

Traditional fish stew eaten by the families of fishermen is more likely to be made with less-prized types of fish, particularly smaller fish that were not able to be sold or were left over at the market at the end of the day. If you live a long distance from the sea you might not have access to fresh seafood, so preserved fish such as salt cod or salted sardines will probably be part of your cooking tradition, or you might opt for legumes, pulses or barnyard animals.

The depth and diversity in the food eaten along the Adriatic coast is not just about regional differences; it can be narrowed down to provinces, towns and even families.

ABOUT ADRIATICO

The recipes in *Adriatico* are the result of a three-month research trip spent travelling the length of the coast and a short distance inland. Many are traditional dishes that I saw on menus or tasted, others are adapted from older cookbooks I found on my travels, and still others are from local people I met along the way, who shared their food and memories with me. Many, especially those from the south, are 'cucina povera' – peasant-style dishes and one-pot meals eaten at a time when using leftovers, from legumes to bread, was the only way there would be enough food to feed the family.

There are seven Italian regions that face the Adriatic coast. The seven chapters of the book do not necessarily reflect individual regions, but describe seven geographic features of the coast. For example, I divided the region of Puglia in two (the Salento peninsula in the south and the Gargano promontory in the north) as, in spite of the similarities, I found many differences in the typical dishes based on historical factors, terrain and climate. It made sense to divide the book into promontories, lagoons and 'riviere' (coastlines) as it is often that particular feature that influences the grains and vegetables that are grown, the barnyard animals that are kept and the way the seafood is traditionally prepared.

Through the pages of this book, I invite you to travel along the scenic Adriatic coastline with me, meeting the people who live close to its shore and tasting the foods they traditionally share.

KITCHEN NOTES

Oven temperatures are for a conventional oven. If you have a fan-forced oven, decrease the temperature by 10–20°C (20–40°F).

Eggs are 60 g (2 oz) and free-range.

Milk is full fat.

Polenta is made from milled dried corn and is usually yellow, although in the Veneto it is sometimes white. I generally use regular polenta rather than the instant kind that has been precooked, dried and processed into a flour, except when I am in a rush or making polenta crostini (see page 227).

To make soft polenta for four, bring 600 ml (21 fl oz) of water to the boil, then reduce the heat to a rolling boil. Pour in 120 g (4 oz) of polenta in a slow steady stream, whisking the whole time. Change the whisk for a wooden spoon, reduce the heat so that the mixture is barely bubbling and give it a good stir; it will be very thick. The whisk ensures you do not get lumps and stirring with the spoon means the polenta won't stick to the base of the pan as it cooks. Polenta takes about 45 minutes to cook, depending on the coarseness of the milled corn. If you are planning on making a firmer polenta, reduce the quantity of water to 500 ml (17 fl oz/2 cups).

Contrary to popular belief, you do not need to stir polenta constantly. If the temperature is low enough and the proportion of liquid to cornmeal is correct, you will only need to stir occasionally so that it does not stick and cooks evenly. I stir it every 3–4 minutes or so after swapping the whisk for the spoon. My mother never measures the polenta; she just adds as much as she needs until the texture looks right. You can add more boiling water at any stage during the cooking to adjust the texture, although you may need to whisk or stir extra hard for a minute to dissolve any lumps that may form.

Some people cook polenta in broth or milk, which gives it a richer flavour. I tend to use water and then, towards the end when it is peeling off the side of the pan, I take it off the heat and stir in a good knob of butter and/or a handful of parmesan, depending on the sauce I will be serving with it.

Semolina is made from the pale yellow heart of durum wheat. When it has been finely ground it is called semolina flour or superfine semolina (semola rimacinata in Italian). It is used in all the fresh pasta recipes in *Adriatico*, either in the dough itself or for dusting freshly made pasta. When added to the pasta dough it adds texture and strength; and when used for dusting, it is less sticky than regular flour so is more effective at keeping the pasta shapes separate before cooking. Coarsely milled semolina can appear quite yellow and is sometimes confused with polenta, which is actually milled dried corn. Regular semolina or polenta flour should not be used as substitutes for superfine semolina (semola rimacinata). At a pinch you can use plain (all-purpose) flour instead, though this is not ideal.

To toast nuts or seeds, spread them out on a baking tray and place in a preheated 180°C (350°F) oven. The cooking time will vary depending on the type of nut or seed and its size, so start checking after 5 minutes and give the tray a bit of shake to look for colour. It should take around 10–15 minutes but be guided by colour and fragrance.

Vincotto (also called 'sapa' or grape must syrup) is the pressed juice of grapes (known as grape must) that has been cooked down slowly to a thick sweet syrup. It is often found in more traditional sweets and cakes as it was used in place of sugar, which was a luxury. I like to add a dash of it as a balancing ingredient in savoury dishes. You can make it at home with different types of wine grapes (either white or red, or a combination) by pressing the juice from the grapes, filtering out the seeds and skin, and cooking it slowly until it has reduced to the desired consistency.

I have found a few types of vincotto in Australia – one that is rich, sweet and sticky, which is just how they make it in Italy, and others that have a small amount of wine vinegar added. The latter are best used as a condiment for savoury dishes or salads. Have a look of the list of ingredients so you know what you're buying; it can be quite expensive but a little goes a long way. I always use the traditional pure vincotto and if I need to balance out the sweetness, I add a bit of balsamic or wine vinegar myself.

SEAFOOD

Seafood can be challenging to clean and fillet if you did not grow up doing it. Luckily, most fishmongers will do the job for you, but there are a few things that are good to know. Here are my tips for cleaning and cooking some of the seafood that appears in Adriatico.

CEPHALOPODS

Cephalopods include calamari, squid, octopus and cuttlefish. They are fluid creatures in the water, either with a cuttlebone for a backbone (cuttlefish), a flexible quill backbone (squid) or none at all (octopus). It is mainly these distinctions that make the cleaning procedures slightly different. All can generally be purchased pre-cleaned from your fishmongers (or they might clean them for you on the spot). Very small and very fresh cephalods usually need little cleaning, if at all.

Cleaning calamari and squid

These have similar backbone configurations so the same cleaning process can be followed for both. If you plan on stuffing them, check to make sure the hood has not been pierced in any way (which can occur during fishing).

Hold the hood with your left hand and the tentacles and head with your right hand. Pull the head and tentacles firmly so they separate from the hood. Remove the beak and trim the tentacles from the head (the tentacles can be eaten and are often used in the dish). Feel inside the hood for the backbone or quill, which will be long, clear and run the entire length of the body. It usually slips out easily. It if is not as long as the body, it has probably broken and will need to be retrieved from the inside of the hood. Remove any remaining guts or broken pieces of quill by rinsing the hood in water and then cleaning the inside with your fingers. The outer coloured skin can also be removed by grabbing one end of it and peeling it back.

Cleaning cuttlefish

Cuttlefish have a broad central white cuttlebone. I used to see these washed up on the beach in Blairgowrie (on the outskirts of Melbourne, Australia) where we spent our summer holidays – I never knew what they were until I started cleaning fish with my father. Cuttlefish have an ink sac that you might like to use in cooking; however, I find that these usually break during the fishing or handling process, leaving the cuttlefish streaked with black. The ink is water-soluble so don't worry about it staining clothes or your benchtop (except if you have one made of untreated wood).

Locate the backbone by feeling along the hood; lay the cuttlefish on your chopping board with the cuttlebone facing up. Break the skin over the top of the bone with the tip of a knife, making sure the incision is large enough to remove the whole bone. Next, hold the hood with your left hand and the tentacles and head with your right hand. Pull the head and tentacles firmly so they separate from the hood. Remove the beak and trim the short tentacles from the head (the tentacles can be eaten and are often used in the dish).

Cooking calamari, squid or cuttlefish

The general rules to follow when cooking cephalods is to cook them briefly (just 2–3 minutes) on a grill, barbecue or in hot oil until they change colour, or slowly, often in a wet braise, for at least 30–45 minutes, depending on the size.

MUSSELS

Cleaning mussels

Mussels have usually already had a preliminary clean prior to being dispensed to fish shops. Discard any broken shells or mussels that are open and do not close when you tap them. Scrub the shells clean one at a time, using a scourer or wire brush and a bit of water. Remove the beards that usually emerge from between the two shells by pulling gently on them and cutting them with small scissors. Place cleaned mussels in a bowl filled with water and give them a good rinse, moving them around the bowl with your hand. Once drained they are ready for use. If you are not going to cook them immediately, place the bowl in the fridge covered with a wet tea towel until you are ready.

Cooking mussels

The simplest way to cook mussels is to steam them open. Place the cleaned mussels in a large lidded frying pan over high heat. Shake the pan after 30 seconds, and then again after a minute. Lift off the lid and, using tongs, remove any mussels that have opened. Replace the lid, give the pan another shake and check again. Repeat for up to 5 minutes, after which time you should discard any mussels that have not opened. When the mussels open they release a flavoursome salty liquid, and you should keep this for any sauces you might be preparing. Sometimes mussels are steamed open in a sauce (such as garlic, parsley and wine); the method for this will be described in the recipe.

CLAMS

Cleaning clams

Clams generally trap sand between the two shell halves as they essentially live in the sand underwater. To clean them, rinse the clams under running water to remove any external sand, then place them in a bowl of salted cold water (add 1 heaped tablespoon of coarse salt for every litre of water). The clams should be well covered by the water. Leave undisturbed for 3 hours, then drain. They are now ready to go, although there is no way of being completely sure all the sand has been removed except by separating the mollusc from its shell.

Cooking clams

Clam shells can be steamed open in much the same way as mussels, although you should keep an eye on the cooking time – if you cook them longer than 10 minutes they are likely to be tough.

PASTA

If there is one food that defines Italy it has to be pasta. At its simplest it is milled wheat and a binding agent (either water
or eggs), mixed and worked to produce a stretchy dough that can be shaped, cut and stuffed dozens of different ways.
I make pasta several times a week – it's one of the things my mother taught me and is a tradition I cherish. Every chapter
in Adriatico has at least one pasta recipe, varying from store-bought to homemade, each one as delicious as the last.

BASIC EQUIPMENT FOR PASTA

You do not need a lot of equipment to make pasta. When I run pasta-making classes, participants are amazed that you can get by with just a rolling pin and a large sharp knife to make thick hand-cut spaghetti. Investing in specific equipment helps you get different thicknesses and shapes, but to make basic spaghetti, you need very little. Here is a list of what I use.

Rolling pin: made of wood and any size that will fit in your pantry.

Pasta board: a board made with untreated wood is very useful but not strictly necessary. It keeps the working area contained and makes cleaning much easier; in addition, the wood is slightly rough, giving the pasta rolled on it a slight texture, meaning the sauce will adhere to it better. The wooden surface is porous so liquids left on the surface will seep into it and discolour or warp it (if there is a lot of liquid). It can't be cleaned with detergents, but rather with a metal pastry scraper (see below) and a slightly damp clean cloth. My boards have dark stains from making pasta with squid ink and red wine that I cannot remove, but I don't mind – they will fade over time.

Pastry scraper: I use a metal scraper with a flat edge for cutting pasta dough (some people use it for mixing as well). It is also very useful for cleaning your wooden board. My scraper has a cut out through which I thread my fingers.

Brush: I have a dedicated paint brush (from the hardware shop) that I use to clean pasta equipment that cannot be washed, such as the hand-cranked machine and the chitarra.

Chitarra/guitar: a chitarra has a wooden frame and many strings across it; when a sheet of pasta is laid across the strings and pressed with a rolling pin, the strands of pasta are cut by the strings themselves. It is usually two-sided, with strings at different widths, enabling you to make narrow or wider spaghetti. You can make the sheet of pasta by rolling it by hand or by rolling it through your pasta machine. A chitarra must be cleaned with a dedicated brush (see left).

Hand-cranked pasta machine: if you want to make ravioli or other filled pasta, a hand-cranked machine is almost essential to roll the pasta into thin sheets. It generally comes with an attachment for cutting the pasta into ribbon-shaped fettuccine. I use an Italian-made machine, one of the more expensive ones with all-metal internal components. I found that in cheaper brands the dial that controls the position of the rollers fails within a fairly short period of time if you use it as often as I do. To clean your pasta machine, use a dedicated brush (see left).

Fluted pastry cutter: this is not essential, but it's an easy and pretty way to cut ravioli and farfalle (butterfly shapes).

Ravioli cutters: these are not essential either, but it's handy to have a selection of round or square cutters for ravioli. They usually have fluted edges that help seal the two layers of pasta together. I use my round cutter quite often but I don't ever use the moulds that are in a tray of 12–15 square ravioli – I find that the ravioli do not separate very easily.

HOW TO MAKE PASTA

The secret to making pasta is getting the proportion of dry and wet ingredients right. When making egg pasta, the basic rule of thumb is one 60 g (2 oz) egg for every 100 g (3½ oz) of flour; for eggless pasta, use around 60 ml (2 fl oz) of water for every 100 g (3½ oz) of flour. However the moisture in the air, the temperature, and the type of flour you use can all affect these proportions, meaning you may need more or less flour to liquid. It all comes down to the feel of the pasta dough as you are working it. For this reason I always make the dough by hand and not in a food processor. Aim for a smooth, elastic dough that is firm and not sticky. The more you make pasta, the better you will become at instinctively knowing the right consistency or texture.

FLOUR

In general, 100 g (3½ oz) of flour or semolina flour is the portion size for one person, so 400 g (14 oz) will be enough for four. If you are making filled pasta like ravioli, anywhere between 50 g (1¾ oz) and 100 g (3½ oz) per person should suffice, though it does depend on your portion size and how much wastage there is when you cut out the shapes.

For most pasta I use plain (all-purpose) flour or soft wheat flour (often labelled as being suitable for making pasta and gnocchi); I do not necessarily use 00 flour, which is finely milled. When making egg-free pasta I use superfine semolina (semola rimacinata) on its own or in combination with 00 or plain flour (I whisk them together before putting them on my work surface). I always dust freshly made pasta and my work surface with superfine semolina when rolling out the pasta.

EGG-FREE PASTA

Although there are no recipes that use egg-free pasta in *Adriatico*, you can easily convert egg pasta to a vegan or egg-free version by using water in place of eggs. Typically fresh egg-free pasta is made using superfine semolina or a equal quantity of 00 or plain (all-purpose) flour and superfine semolina, but you can also make it with just plain flour. The result will not be as rich without the eggs and will look strangely pale if you don't use semolina, but it will still work.

To make it, place a mound of semolina or flour on your work surface and make a well in the centre. Add a couple of tablespoons of water to the well, using your fingertips or the tines of a fork to incorporate the water into the semolina or flour on the edges of the well. Then, if you are making coloured pasta, add the colouring ingredient (such as squid ink or finely chopped blanched spinach) and a bit more water, and work that in. By now you will need to work the dough with your fingertips. Add more water, and keep working in the semolina or flour in an ever-widening circle until you have used up most of the semolina or flour and have a smooth but firm elastic dough. Knead for 5 minutes. Cover with an upturned bowl and allow to rest for at least 30 minutes, then roll out and shape as desired.

EGG PASTA

Place a mound of flour on your work surface and make a well in the centre. Crack the eggs into the well (and, if using, your colouring ingredient, such as squid ink or finely chopped blanched spinach) and start whisking the eggs gently with the tines of a fork, incorporating a bit of flour at the same time. Keep whisking with the fork, making an ever-widening circle as you incorporate more flour. The mixture will eventually become too thick for you to use the fork so start using your fingertips, working the wet ingredients into the dry ingredients until you have used up most of the dry ingredients and a ball of dough forms. You may need to add a bit of water or flour to get the right consistency. Knead for about 5 minutes until it is smooth and elastic. Cover with an upturned bowl and allow to rest for at least 30 minutes, then roll out and shape as desired.

USING A PASTA MACHINE TO MAKE FRESH PASTA SHEETS

After your dough has rested, dust your work surface with superfine semolina. Cut off a portion of dough (about 100 g/3½ oz) and keep the rest of the dough covered. Roll out the dough with a rolling pin until it is thin enough to go through the widest setting of your pasta machine. Thread it through the rollers of the machine, turning the handle to make the rollers move. Allow the pasta sheet to drop from the machine. Fold the rolled sheet in half, dust it with superfine semolina if it is sticky, and give the sheet a quarter turn before threading it through the machine again. The quarter turn means that the pasta is going through the machine in a different direction and is essentially being kneaded. As you continue to fold, roll and turn the dough, the gluten will start to work and the dough will become firmer. Repeat as many times as needed to make the dough lose much of its stretch (usually five or six times). Try to keep the dough in a rectangular shape, especially at the end of this process; you may need to use the rolling pin to help you shape it.

Once the dough has become firm, you can start turning the dial of the machine to bring the rollers closer together, rolling the dough thinner each time. You no longer need to give the dough a quarter turn and you only need to roll it through each setting once. Dust the pasta sheets with superfine semolina if the dough sticks to the machine as it goes through. Repeat until your pasta reaches the desired thickness.

Once you have made your pasta sheets or shapes, dust your work surface as well as the sheets/shapes with more superfine semolina. To prevent the pasta from drying out, cover it with a clean tea towel until you are ready to use it.

1

LA PENISOLA SALENTINA

The tip of the heel and southern-most part of the boot of the Italian peninsula is known as the Salento. This finger of land is bathed by the sea on three sides, and juts out into the Mediterranean Sea at the fishing town of Santa Maria di Leuca. It has been invaded many times over thousands of years: the Greeks, the Byzantines, the Aragonese and the Bourbons are among those who left traces of their presence in the culture, language and food of the area.

The locals are known as Salentini and although the area is part of the region of Puglia, the local dialect is quite different from Pugliese which is spoken in the north; it has Spanish, French and Greek influences, with some groups in the centre of the peninsula speaking 'Griko', a dialect which is more like Greek than Italian. The Messapic people, probably arriving from Crete, were in the Salento before the Romans, and are said to have brought olives, vines and horses to the area, and made terracotta pots and urns for wine and olive oil from the local red clay. In fact, horse meat is still eaten in the traditional dish 'pezzetti di cavallo', where pieces of meat are cooked slowly in a clay pot on the hearth with onions and tomatoes. The Greek legacy continues to be felt with vines and especially olives, which not only dominate the landscape but also the economy of the Salento.

Up until the 1900s, the peninsula was the domain of a few rich landowners and the many who worked the land and lived in poverty. The relative isolation of the Salento meant that, apart from the influence of the historical invasions, the traditional cooking methods were maintained. Food was prepared with produce that was grown locally and readily available. Vegetables form the basis of many traditional dishes, a type of 'cucina povera' (peasant cooking), with meat dishes reserved for special celebrations.

Traditional dishes often contain leftovers. 'Cecamariti' (husband blinders) is a typical peasant dish, made with broken chunks of stale bread fried in olive oil, mixed with cooked broad (fava) beans or chickpeas from an earlier meal. This recycled dish is meant to trick or 'blind' husbands to the fact that it is made entirely out of leftovers.

When I travelled south from Brindisi towards Otranto I was struck by a relative absence of industry; the area is rural and agricultural. The ruddy earth is dotted with silvery olive trees, often with broad and torturous trunks. There are almonds, vines and prickly pears, with fields bordered by 'muretti a secco' (low dry stone walls that divide the land and form the perimeter of properties) as well as occasional 'furnieddhu', a round dry stone dwelling used as a shelter from the heat. And then there is the bluest sea encasing the whole peninsula.

The towns of Leuca, Otranto and Brindisi are the main fishing ports of the Adriatic coast in the Salento, together with the smaller fishing township of Tricase. I'd been told that traditional fishing is becoming increasingly rare; that small

boats called 'gozzi' were not used anymore and the practice of fishing equipment being handed down from father to son in fishing families was dying out. When I visited Santa Maria di Leuca, a number of smallish boats were moored to the pier, next to piles of colourful woven nets and benches with signs where fishermen had laid out the night's catch for sale, so I like to think there is still a small traditional fishing trade. In the town at a trattoria overlooking the water, we ate the freshest marinated anchovies, the most tender grilled squid, and the sweetest fried prawns; the waiter told us that the seafood had been fished by a local fisherman, and pointed to the pier down below.

Fresh seafood is best cooked simply – grilled, fried or just marinated, with a good drizzling of Salento olive oil to highlight the freshness of the seafood. Traditionally, fishermen and their families ate the least-valued varieties of fish, such as sardines and mackerel, and would conserve some of their catch through salting or drying to use when fresh fish was not available. Typical dishes of the area use mussels, calamari or squid, sardines or dried cod (called 'stoccafisso').

Cheeses in southern Italy are predominantly made from sheep's milk, and occasionally goat's milk. This is also true of the Salento, where the terrain and climate favour small-hoofed animals and typical cheeses are sheep's milk ricotta, cacioricotta, 'ricotta forte' (spreadable aged ricotta with an intense flavour) and pecorino at various stages of aging.

The types of breads and pasta eaten in the Salento reflect the rurality and relative poverty of the people. Frise or friselle are often found on traditional tables in the Salento; the small round loaves are partially baked until firm on the outside, cut in half horizontally with a metal string (giving them a textured surface) and baked again until dry and crisp, making them last almost indefinitely. In Otranto I stopped to buy green leafy vegetables from a man who was unloading them, still with roots and dirt attached, from the boot of his car. His wife asked me if I wanted to try her friselle, which she'd made in her outdoor wood-fired oven. 'Sì grazie,' I thanked her, and she pulled out a bag full of thick golden bangles of twice-cooked bread. 'You have to dip them in water before eating,' she advised, 'then top them with ripe tomatoes, oregano and "un buon olio d'oliva del Salento" (a good-quality local olive oil).' I did exactly that and they tasted amazing.

Pasta is made without eggs, often using coarse flour and water, and the typical shapes of the region are 'orecchiette' (literally 'little ears' due to their shape). Sauces are simple, often vegan and again doused liberally with golden local oil.

The simple food of the Salento wouldn't be the same without an accompanying glass of local wine, which is predominantly red (Negroamaro and Primitivo) or a clean, crisp glass of the local white, Verdeca.

Melanzane ripiene con le sarde
Stuffed eggplants with sardines

Sardines are one of the most abundant fish found in the Adriatic. Nothing makes me happier than seeing silvery sardines piled high at the fish market – even better if they have been freshly filleted, meaning a lot less work at home. Eggplants (aubergines) and sardines make very good partners, and 'marangiane', which is what the locals call eggplants ('melanzane' in Italian), are abundant in the dry summers of the Salento. Medium to small eggplants make a superb summer starter when stuffed with a flavoursome mix of sardines, capers, garlic and herbs.

Soaking fresh sardine fillets in vinegar is something I picked up from my Sicilian friend Jessica, who lives in Milan. She told me that soaking them removes the strong fishy flavour, and it also gives the dish that savoury sour balance, which works really well with the basil and mint. So although this recipe is based on one from Maria Rosaria's book on the Salento (see page 34), it has personalised touches from other parts of Italy.

120 g (4 oz) sardine fillets

125 ml (4 fl oz/½ cup) white wine vinegar

2 medium eggplants (aubergines)

1 tablespoon salted capers, soaked in water for 10 minutes, drained

1 clove garlic, crushed

2 anchovy fillets, chopped

1 tablespoon chopped basil leaves, plus extra whole leaves to garnish

1 tablespoon chopped mint leaves

2 tablespoons dried breadcrumbs

sea salt

splash of extra virgin olive oil

Place the sardine fillets in a small bowl with the vinegar and allow them to soak for about an hour. Drain and rinse well, then pat dry and finely chop. Set aside.

Preheat the oven to 180°C (350°F).

Bring a saucepan of salted water to the boil. Cut the eggplants in half lengthways and plunge them in the water. Allow the water to return to the boil and cook for a couple of minutes, then drain. If your eggplants are larger, you may need to cook them a bit longer.

Scoop the flesh out of the eggplants, leaving a 3–5 mm (¼ in) shell, with a bit more at the stalk end. Finely chop the flesh and place in a bowl with the chopped sardine fillets and the drained capers, garlic, anchovy, basil, mint, half the breadcrumbs and salt to taste. Mix well, then spoon the filling into the eggplant halves and scatter evenly with the remaining breadcrumbs.

Drizzle a little olive oil in the base of a baking dish and add the eggplant halves, fitting them snugly in a single layer. Add a little water to the dish so it is about 5 mm (¼ in) deep.

Bake for 40 minutes or until the tops of the eggplants are golden and the flesh is soft. Garnish with extra basil leaves and serve warm, or set them aside and enjoy them later at room temperature.

SERVES 4 AS A STARTER

Cozze piccanti
Spicy marinated mussels

Maria Rosaria's book La Cucina Salentina *on cooking in the Salento is a lovely exploration of the heart of the people of this region. It is filled with hand-drawn images of scenes from days long gone and recipes that have been handed down within families. This recipe is based on one that I found in the book. I first tried it when we were staying in Otranto – I'd bought the mussels from the local 'pescheria' (fish shop) and the shop owner told me they'd been fished from the sea that very day.*

Plump mussels are cooked briefly in garlic, chilli, anchovies and a splash of vinegar, then allowed to rest overnight to soak up the flavours. Eat them as an appetiser with toothpicks, accompanied by a glass of chilled local white, Verdeca.

You will need to start this recipe one day ahead

600 g (1 lb 5 oz) fresh mussels, cleaned and debearded (see page 17)

1½ tablespoons extra virgin olive oil

1 clove garlic, crushed

1 small dried chilli

2 anchovies, small bones removed

3 tablespoons dry white wine

3 tablespoons white wine vinegar

1–2 tablespoons chopped flat-leaf parsley, plus extra leaves to serve (optional)

toasted bread rounds, to serve (optional)

Place a large frying pan with a lid over medium–high heat. Add the mussels in a single layer, then cover and cook for about 2 minutes, shaking the pan every 30 seconds or so. Remove the open shells and set aside. Replace the lid and cook the remaining mussels for another 30 seconds, then check again for open shells and remove those that have opened. Repeat a few more times, then discard any unopened shells after 5 minutes.

Using a small sharp knife, separate the mussel meat from the open shells at the base of the stalk. Discard the shells and pat the mussel meat dry (or drain well in a colander).

Place the olive oil, garlic and chilli in a frying pan that will fit all the mussels. Heat over medium heat until the garlic becomes fragrant, then add the mussels, anchovies, wine, vinegar and parsley. Increase the heat to medium–high and allow most of the liquid to evaporate (it should only take a few minutes). Tip the mussels and remaining liquid into a small ceramic bowl. Allow to cool, then cover and place in the fridge overnight.

The next day, allow the mussels come to room temperature, and scatter with extra parsley (if using). Serve the mussels on their own with small forks or toothpicks, or on small rounds of toasted bread.

SERVES 4 AS AN APPETISER

Pomodori scattarisciati
'Popped' tomatoes

Fruit and vegetables are best eaten when they are in season as they will taste the way they are meant to taste. I find this to be particularly true for tomatoes, which now seem to be available all year round – they are bland and watery in winter and not worth the expense. Tomatoes are at their sweet best in late summer, when the hot sun has brought out their rich flavour and natural sugars. In the Salento, a simple way of eating cherry tomatoes that are in danger of becoming overripe is to put them in a pan and allow the heat to 'pop' their skins and release their juices, which mingle deliciously with the garlicky olive oil and salty capers. Serve pomodori scattarisciati on a summer evening with plenty of bread to mop up the sweet, salty pan juices. You could even eat them with a plate of pasta – orecchiette would be ideal.

2 tablespoons extra virgin
olive oil

1 clove garlic, sliced

500 g (1 lb 2 oz) very ripe
cherry tomatoes

2 tablespoons salted capers,
soaked in water for 10 minutes,
drained

½ teaspoon dried oregano

½ teaspoon chilli flakes,
or to taste

sea salt

crusty or day-old bread,
to serve

Place the olive oil and garlic in a large frying pan with a lid over medium–high heat. Add the tomatoes when the garlic becomes fragrant and cover with the lid. Allow to cook for a couple of minutes, shaking the pan occasionally, until the tomatoes 'pop' their skins. Help any tomatoes that haven't popped by flattening them slightly with the back of a wooden spoon.

Add the capers and oregano and replace the lid. Reduce the heat to low and cook for another 20 minutes or until the tomatoes are softened but still retain their shape, and have released their lovely juices into the pan. Add the chilli flakes and a good pinch of salt.

Serve directly from the pan while the tomatoes are still warm, offering plenty of bread to mop up the juices

SERVES 6

Orecchiette con salsicca e cime di rapa
Orecchiette with sausage and broccoli rabe

There are a number of streets in the old part of the town of Bari where you will see ladies sitting at tables making orecchiette pasta with enviable ease. The word 'orecchiette' means 'little ears', named for their typical shape, made by dragging a circle of dough over a slightly rough work surface. Although Bari is not strictly part of the Salento, this shape of pasta is very typical of the whole of Puglia, including the Salento. Orecchiette are commonly cooked with broccoli rabe (cime di rapa), and they are often served with 'poor man's cheese' (dried breadcrumbs fried in olive oil). However, I like to mix it up a bit and sometimes add anchovies for a salty kick or, as I have here, pork sausages to make the dish more substantial.

1 bunch broccoli rabe
(or use broccolini)

2 good-quality pure pork
sausages

2 tablespoons extra virgin olive
oil, plus extra to serve

1 clove garlic, finely chopped

good pinch of chilli flakes

400 g (14 oz) orecchiette

grated aged pecorino, to serve

Wash and trim the base of the broccoli rabe stems, then cut into 5–6 cm (2–2½ in) pieces, separating the leafy tips from the stems. Discard the thicker stems, reserving the finer stems.

Remove the skins from the sausages and tear the meat into bite-sized chunks.

Heat the olive oil in a large frying pan over medium heat, add the sausage meat and cook until it is coloured all over. Add the garlic and chilli and cook until fragrant, then add the broccoli rabe tips. Reduce the heat to low and cook for a few minutes or until the green tips have wilted.

Meanwhile, bring a large saucepan of salted water to the boil and drop in the reserved broccoli rabe stems. After 2 minutes, add the orecchiette and cook until al dente, following the instructions on the packet. Drain, reserving a little of the pasta water in a cup. Drop the orecchiette and broccoli rabe stems into the frying pan and toss them through the sauce, adding some of the reserved pasta water if it looks a bit dry.

Serve immediately, drizzled with extra virgin olive oil and a generous sprinkling of pecorino.

SERVES 4

Tiella di patate e carciofi di Enrica
Enrica's potato and artichoke bake

Many dishes of the Salento peninsula are vegan, using the seasonal abundance to make tasty meals that don't require any meat or dairy. In spring, when the fields are bursting with small purple artichokes, a delicious way of eating them is a 'tiella' ('taieddha' or 'taieddra' in the local dialect). The word refers to the earthenware dish in which the food is baked, although it is used interchangeably with the food made within it. It is essentially a one-pot layered bake and the most traditional tiella in Puglia is made with layers of potatoes, mussels and rice (see page 86). To make matters slightly confusing, the word 'tiella' is also used in other regions to describe other types of dishes made in the same type of pot, but let's not dwell on that!

Signora Enrica, a passionate cook of dishes from the Salento, gave me this recipe when I was staying with her last spring. I asked her for her favourite artichoke recipe, since I had bought far too many from a mobile vegetable seller in the small town of Uggiano. She was happy to, although she didn't so much give me the recipe as list the ingredients while we were having a chat. Trimming artichokes can be a lot of work and if this bothers you, the dish works equally well with frozen artichokes. I was tempted to add a bit of aged pecorino to the breadcrumb and olive oil crust when I first made it, and sort of hoped Enrica had forgotten to mention the cheese when she listed the ingredients, but honestly, it just doesn't need it.

1 lemon (if you are using fresh artichokes)

6–8 medium artichokes (or 500 g/1 lb 2 oz frozen artichokes)

3 large potatoes

extra virgin olive oil, for drizzling

1 clove garlic, crushed

2 tablespoons chopped flat-leaf parsley, plus extra to serve

1 tablespoon salted capers, soaked in water for 10 minutes, drained

2 tablespoons black olives (preferably from the Salento), pitted and halved

1 x 400 g (14 oz) tin roma (plum) tomatoes, drained and roughly chopped

sea salt

100 g (3½ oz/1 cup) dried breadcrumbs

finely grated zest of 1 lemon (optional)

To clean the artichokes, fill a large bowl with water and squeeze in the juice from the lemon, dropping the lemon halves in the water as well. Cut off most of the stalk from each artichoke, leaving about 2 cm (¾ in) at the top. Remove the tough outer leaves, the outer part of the top of the stalk and the top part of the leaves. Essentially, you need to remove all the tough or bitter parts of the flower. Remove the hairy choke with a teaspoon and cut the remaining artichoke heart into quarters, then each quarter into thin wedges. Keep the prepared artichokes in the acidulated water until you are ready to use them.

If you are using frozen artichokes that have already been cleaned, just cut them into thin wedges.

Preheat the oven to 180°C (350°F).

Peel the potatoes and cut them into slices that are slightly thicker than the artichokes.

To assemble the tiella, you will need a 24 cm (9½ in) round or square baking dish or cake tin, or similar. Drizzle the base with olive oil and scatter over some of the garlic. Place a single layer of potato slices on the base, then a layer of artichoke slices. Scatter over half the parsley, half the capers, half the olives and half the tomato, followed by a dash of olive oil, the remaining garlic and a light sprinkling of salt. Add another layer of potato, then the rest of the artichoke, parsley, capers, olives and tomato. Finish with a final layer of potato.

Pour enough water into the dish or tin to come just over halfway up the side. If you are using frozen artichokes that release liquid, you won't need as much water – just pour in enough to come about one-third of the way up.

Place the breadcrumbs in a bowl and add gradually add olive oil until the crumbs clump together. Scatter the crumbs generously over the potato layer, then cover with foil and bake for 1 hour. After this time, check the vegetables with a fork – they should be tender and cooked through. If they are still firm bake for another 5–10 minutes, then check again. When they are ready, remove the foil and bake for 5–10 minutes, until the breadcrumb topping is golden.

Scatter over the lemon zest (if using) and extra parsley, and serve hot or warm as a side dish with oven-baked fish or as a vegan main meal.

SERVES 4 AS A MAIN OR 6 AS A SIDE DISH

Baccalà al forno con patate alla Salentina
Baked salted cod with potatoes

Baccalà is preserved salted cod and has a reputation for having quite a fishy smell. I remember seeing it in the Italian deli I used to visit with my parents, slabs of oddly folded fillets covered in coarse salt sitting in open boxes on the bench. Stockfish is the air-dried spidery-looking version of cod, often kept hanging on the deli wall. I have grown to love baccalà, although I admit I was well into my adulthood before I tried cooking with it. It can be quite rewarding – you just have to give it the time it needs to bring it back to life.

We all have busy lives, so reducing the soaking and preparation time is a good thing, and I recently found 'wet' baccalà still covered in salt but pre-soaked. It still requires some soaking, but this is more to remove the excess salt as it is already quite moist. If you can't find pre-soaked baccalà, increase the soaking time to up to 2 days, until it feels like firm fresh fish, making sure you change the water at least every 12 hours. The baccalà remains quite salty, so this dish needs no added salt, but the potatoes give a nice starchy balance.

500 g (1 lb 2 oz) wet baccalà

1 red capsicum (pepper)

1 small onion, thinly sliced

100 ml (3½ fl oz) extra virgin olive oil

35 g (1¼ oz/⅓ cup) dried breadcrumbs

500 g (1 lb 2 oz) potatoes, peeled and thinly sliced

1 teaspoon dried oregano

freshly ground black pepper

6 cherry tomatoes, quartered

30–40 small black olives

2 tablespoons grated aged pecorino

1 tablespoon finely chopped oregano

Place the wet baccalà in a large bowl of water and soak for 4 hours, changing the water two or three times. Taste a small piece of flesh; if it is still excessively salty, soak it for a bit longer. It should still be salty, but edible. Drain and pat dry, then remove the skin, fins and bones and break the flesh into bite-sized chunks.

Preheat the oven to 200°C (400°F) and line a baking tray with baking paper.

Cut the capsicum in half lengthways and remove the stem and seeds. Place in the oven and roast for 20–30 minutes, until the skin is charred and the flesh is soft. Place in a plastic bag for a minute or so to allow the capsicum to sweat, then remove and peel off the charred skin. Don't wash it or you will lose the lovely smoky flavour. Cut the flesh into strips about 5 mm (¼ in) wide. Leave the oven on.

Finely dice one-third of the thinly sliced onion and set aside.

Drizzle 2 tablespoons of olive oil in the base of a medium baking dish and sprinkle evenly with 2 tablespoons of the breadcrumbs. Now layer in the ingredients in the following order: half the potato slices, the sliced onion, the capsicum strips, half the dried oregano, the cod, the diced onion, a good grinding of pepper, the remaining potato slices, the tomatoes, the olives and the rest of the dried oregano. Drizzle with 2 tablespoons of olive oil, then scatter with the remaining breadcrumbs mixed with the pecorino.

Bake for 45 minutes or until the top is golden. Allow to cool for 5 minutes before serving. Mix the finely chopped oregano with the last tablespoon of olive oil and drizzle over the baccalà bake.

SERVES 4

Pizza di carciofi e ricotta
Artichoke and ricotta pie

Signora Enrica was born in Otranto and lived there most of her life, only moving to Lecce quite recently. She comes back to Otranto for celebrations like Christmas, when the whole family gets together to cook. At Easter she traditionally makes an artichoke and ricotta covered pie (which she called a 'pizza'), when local green and purple artichokes are plentiful. As we sat in her kitchen in the week leading up to Easter she gave me a vague list of ingredients and methodology, which I jotted down on a scrap of paper. I loved the sound of this festive vegetarian pie, a celebration of spring and its fresh produce. The soft lemony ricotta makes a lovely contrast to the slightly bitter artichokes.

If you don't want to make your own pastry, a good-quality bought short-crust pastry will do the trick nicely. And if you can't find sheep's milk ricotta, cow's milk ricotta makes a respectable substitute. The ricotta should be drained in a sieve for a day before using as it needs to be quite dry.

1 lemon

8–10 medium artichokes
(you will 600 g/1 lb 5 oz
cleaned artichokes)

2 tablespoons extra virgin
olive oil

1 clove garlic, finely chopped

2½ tablespoons white wine

sea salt and freshly ground
black pepper

300 g (10½ oz) fresh ricotta
(ideally sheep's milk), drained
overnight

finely grated zest of 1 lemon

100 g (3½ oz) aged pecorino,
grated

1 egg, lightly beaten

Pastry

400 g (14 oz/2⅔ cups) plain
(all-purpose) flour

1 teaspoon salt

200 g (7 oz) chilled unsalted
butter, cut into small cubes

100 ml (3½ fl oz) chilled water

To make the pastry, place the flour and salt in a large bowl and give it a whisk to remove any lumps. Add the butter and work it into the flour with your fingertips until it resembles wet sand. Add the chilled water and bring the dough together, kneading it briefly. Wrap it plastic film and rest in the fridge for an hour or so.

To clean the artichokes, fill a large bowl with water and squeeze in the juice from the lemon, dropping the lemon halves in the water as well. Cut off most of the stalk from each artichoke, leaving about 2 cm (¾ in) at the top. Remove the tough outer leaves, the outer part of the top of the stalk and the top part of the leaves. Essentially you need to remove all the tough or bitter parts of the flower. Remove the hairy choke with a teaspoon and cut the remaining artichoke heart into quarters, then each quarter into thin wedges. Store the prepared artichokes in the acidulated water until you are ready to use them.

Heat the olive oil in a large frying pan over medium heat. Add the garlic and cook until fragrant, then add the drained artichokes and toss to heat through. Increase the heat to high, add the wine and let it bubble away until it has evaporated. Season to taste with salt and pepper. Reduce the heat to medium–low and cook for a further 5 minutes or until the artichokes start to soften. Remove from the heat and allow to cool.

Put the ricotta through a potato ricer or fine sieve to remove any lumps. Add the lemon zest and pecorino and mix well.

Line the base and side of a 23 cm (9 in) high-rise pie tin or a deep 23 cm springform tin.

Remove the pastry from the fridge and cut into two portions – you need two-thirds of the dough for the base and side, and one-third for the lid. I always roll pastry between two sheets of plastic film. Roll out the larger portion of dough to a thickness of 3–4 mm (⅛ in), to form a circle large enough to line the base and side of the tin. It should hang slightly over the edge as you will need to fold it over the pastry lid later. Carefully lift the pastry into the prepared tin, using your fingers to gently flatten it onto the base and side. Place in the fridge to chill for 15 minutes if the pastry is becoming soft.

Preheat the oven to 200°C (400°F).

Arrange the cooled artichokes over the pastry base and flatten with the back of a spoon. Spoon on the ricotta mixture and again flatten with the back of a spoon.

Roll out the smaller piece of dough to a thickness of 3–4 mm (⅛ in), making a circle that just covers the top of the pie. Place the pastry lid on the filling and fold over the pastry from the side of the tin so it forms a seal. Trim off any excess with a sharp knife. Cut an incision or hole in the centre of the pie lid to help any steam escape during baking. Brush the egg over the pie top.

Bake for 45 minutes or until the pastry is cooked and golden. Allow to cool for about 10 minutes before removing from the tin. Serve warm or at room temperature.

SERVES 8

Pomodori ripieni di riso
Tomatoes stuffed with rice and herbs

Ripe tomatoes are at their best in the late summer, when the aroma of these red jewels fill the gardens of the Salentini. For this recipe you will need to find large just-ripe tomatoes so that you can cut off their tops, scoop out their juicy red innards and replace them with a flavour-packed rice filling. Make sure the tomatoes are quite firm so they maintain their shape when you cook them. I like to use a bit of dried mint in addition to the other herbs in this recipe, as a nod to the Greeks who once lived on the peninsula.

150 g (5½ oz/¾ cup) short-grain rice

8 large ripe but firm tomatoes

3 tablespoons salted capers, soaked in water for 10 minutes, drained

8 large black olives, pitted and chopped

40 g (1½ oz/½ cup) grated aged pecorino

good pinch of chilli flakes

1 teaspoon dried oregano

½ teaspoon dried mint

1 tablespoon chopped flat-leaf parsley

1 tablespoon chopped basil

sea salt and freshly ground black pepper

2 tablespoons olive oil

green salad, to serve

Preheat the oven to 180°C (350°F).

Bring a medium saucepan of water to the boil, add the rice and cook for 5 minutes or until it is half-cooked, then drain and rinse under cold water. Drain again and set aside until you are ready to use it.

Plunge the tomatoes into a saucepan of salted boiling water, then remove immediately and rinse under cold water. Slice off the tops to make lids and scoop out the contents of each tomato, leaving a 1 cm (½ in) shell. Discard the liquid and seeds, but chop the tomato flesh and add it to the cooled rice. Add the capers, olives, cheese, chilli and herbs. Season to taste with salt and pepper and mix well, then spoon the mixture evenly into the tomatoes, taking care not to overfill them as the rice will swell as it continues to cook. Pop the lids on.

Choose a roasting tin that will fit all the tomatoes and place them snugly in one layer. Drizzle with the olive oil.

Cover with foil and bake for 15 minutes, then remove the foil and cook for another 15 minutes or until the tomatoes are tender when checked with a fork and the rice is cooked. The exact cooking time will depend on the size of your tomatoes and their ripeness, so they may take longer. Eat warm or at room temperature, with a green salad.

SERVES 4

Tiella di verdure
Vegetable tiella

One-pot baked dishes are a cook's dream; once you have assembled all the layers there is little else to do. Rather than being a traditional tiella, this is more of a 'leftover vegetable' tiella, using what I had in the fridge and running with the whole tiella concept that is so popular in the Salento. I added aged pecorino to a few of the layers, but you could easily omit the cheese and make the dish vegan. You could also swap pecorino for parmesan if you prefer, and of course you can change the vegetables to fit in with what you happen to have in the fridge – just remember to slice them thinly.

This makes a wonderful accompaniment to a main meal of fish either cooked whole in the oven in a salt crust (see page 200) or on the barbecue (see page 92). There will be lots of cooking juices left in the pan, so make sure you serve plenty of crusty bread on the side.

2 cloves garlic, crushed

3 tablespoons finely chopped flat-leaf parsley, plus extra to garnish

125 ml (4 fl oz/½ cup) extra virgin olive oil

1 small onion, thinly sliced

2 small celery stalks, thinly sliced

3 medium zucchini (courgettes), thinly sliced

sea salt

½ teaspoon fennel seeds, toasted

3 medium tomatoes, thinly sliced

50 g (1¾ oz/⅓ cup) black olives, pitted and halved

100 g (3½ oz) cabbage, thinly sliced

1 large potato, very thinly sliced

2 tablespoons dried breadcrumbs

60 g (2 oz/¾ cup) grated pecorino or parmesan

14 zucchini (courgette) flowers, washed, stamens removed and opened flat

crusty bread, to serve

Preheat the oven to 200°C (400°F).

Mix together the garlic, parsley and 100 ml (3½ fl oz) of the olive oil in a small bowl and set aside.

Drizzle the remaining olive oil over the base of a large round baking dish (mine has a diameter of 30 cm/12 in). Layer in the ingredients in the following order: half the onion, half the celery, half the zucchini, half the garlic and parsley oil, salt to taste, half the fennel seeds, half the tomato, half the olives, half the cabbage, half the potato, half the breadcrumbs, half the grated cheese, then salt to taste. Repeat the layers once more, finishing with grated cheese and salt, then cover the dish with foil and bake for 30 minutes.

Arrange the zucchini flowers around the border and cover again with foil. Bake for another 20–30 minutes, then remove the foil and bake for 10 minutes. Check the potatoes are cooked through – if not, put the dish back in the oven for a further 5–10 minutes.

Scatter with extra parsley and serve with crusty bread to mop up the juices.

SERVES 6 AS A SUBSTANTIAL SIDE DISH

OLIVE OIL
THE GOLD OF THE SALENTO

The recipes of the Salento were born on the stone hearths of the region's peasant farmers. They were an enduring creative answer to want and need, to weather and climate, to soil and sea that, at times, could withhold their bounty for an entire season or release it with abundance. But amidst this uncertainty, there has always been one sure thing in the Salento: its olive oil.

OLIVE OIL
THE GOLD OF THE SALENTO

A last-minute drizzle of olive oil on slow-cooked dried broad (fava) beans and greens turns the simplest of meals into a spectacular dish. Some call the oil from the Salento its gold, both for its colour and its flavour.

Olive oil has an incredibly long history in the area, bound to the story of the land where the ancient olive trees grow, and the people whose very lives have depended on the collection of olives and the making of its oil.

Historians have found evidence that olive oil was made in the Salento as far back as 1300 BC. The warm, dry summer and mild winter are ideal for olives; some of the trees I drove past on the way to the white-walled town of Ostuni had massive twisting trunks, many of them hundreds of years old. In Roman times, Pliny the Elder wrote that the oil produced in southern Italy surpassed the quality of that from Greece. It was shipped from the port of Brindisi to the wider Mediterranean, including Egypt; remnants of amphorae bearing the mark of artisan ceramic producers from the area lie on the floor of the Adriatic Sea, a silent marker of the ships that were wrecked as they sailed with their cargo of oil and wine, and to the ships' Pugliesi origin.

Over time, the role and importance of olives and olive oil in the Salento has waxed and waned; for periods, wine and viticulture were favoured, so olive oil production declined and olive groves were abandoned, only to be revived at a later time. But wars, feuds and chaos over the centuries took their toll on what was a fledgling industry. The end of the 1800s saw many challenges: an increased use of sunflower oil as an alternative for cooking,

the expansion of the world market for olive oil, and unfavourable weather patterns all made it more lucrative for growers to cut down their trees and sell them for fuel, thereby removing the opportunity for ongoing livelihood and that connection with the land and its history.

A leading historian of the tale of Salento and its olive oil, Rina Durante, wrote in her book *L'Oro del Salento* that the mercantile olive oil producers of Italy's north and France rapidly overtook the Salentini, not only in tonnes of oil produced but also in the flavour of the product. Their advantage? The best equipment, minds and new techniques. The producers of the Salento, so distant from the urgency of change and the driving competition that was consuming and transforming the north, fell behind. It was only in the 1900s that the industry saw a turnaround.

Up to the 1800s, oil in the Salento was made in underground grottos that were converted to form oil presses called 'trappeti'. The olives that had fallen on the ground were gathered first; then labourers would shake the trees, trying to coax the remaining olives to let go. The trappeto maintains a constant temperature, always above 6°C (43°F). This makes it an ideal environment for processing as anything below this temperature would cause the oil to solidify.

Workers (trapettari) would labour from October through to March or April, eating and sleeping underground, sometimes side by side with horses and donkeys that helped them carry out the back-breaking work. Olives were crushed in rotary stone presses, largely unchanged

from those used in Roman times. A stone bowl and rounded orbis rotated to press the olives and squeeze out their golden liquid. Much later, screw presses were added, and now electric oil presses with grinders and centrifuges are used to make olive oil. They are usually run by 'aziende agricole' (farming businesses) or 'agriturismi' (farming businesses with a tourism component).

I met Deni Settembre from Azienda Agricola Settembre just outside the town of Otranto. It was April, and although olive season had ended and the trees were bare of fruit, the storage tanks were brimming with oil, as bottling and packaging continues throughout the year. As she showed me around some of the 3500 olive trees on the property, she talked about the Salento having 'a culture of olive trees'.

Deni went on to explain a bit about the different oils, particularly the most prized and expensive of them all – extra virgin olive oil. Acidity is one of the key factors in determining whether an oil is extra virgin or not, and the level of acidity depends on many factors, including the timing of the harvest and the presence or absence of olive fruit flies. To be labelled extra virgin, the acidity level must be no more than 0.8%, the olives must be processed within 24 hours of picking, and they must be cold-pressed (heated to no more than 27°C/80°F). Naturally, the oil should also have a pleasant taste and aroma.

Olive oils can be tasted much like wines can, as soon as they are produced. As Deni explained, ultimately we should be guided by what tastes and smells good to us, as well as considering how we plan to use the oil. For example, a delicate oil is lovely for dressing seafood and a stronger, more floral one is better paired with bitter greens, such as chicory.

Often tasters will look for the 'pizzico' (pepperiness), which indicates that the oil is fresh and usually high-quality extra virgin. During a visit to the organic De Padova Frantoio in Avetrana in full season, I was able to taste the 'pizzico' of the freshly pressed extra virgin oil directly from the tap, where it was flowing thick and green. Owner Francesco told me that this was the source of life, 'la fonte della vita'. The grassy aroma of fresh olive oil filled the 'frantoio' (oil mill) as I walked through, past the dozens of crates of freshly picked green and black fruit waiting to be processed.

There is a myth about colour, which can vary from greenish to golden yellow. Contrary to what some believe, it does not affect flavour and cannot be used to judge quality. Virgin oil has an acidity level of 0.9–2%, but anything higher than this results in oil that is referred to as 'lampante'. This often has an unpleasant taste and odour, but can be treated chemically and mixed with other virgin or extra virgin oil prior to being bottled and sold.

Back in Otranto, Deni told me that when Azienda Agricola Settembre is not in full swing, the neighbouring farmers use their olive presses to make oil from their own olives for personal use; this happens for most if not all olive oil presses in the Salento. Most properties, even those a 10-minute walk from the centre of Otranto, had rows of olive trees with thin silvery leaves planted in the front garden, in blocks next to houses and lining most of the roads. It was just like Deni said earlier: the culture of olive trees and olive oil, right there in people's gardens, a daily fact of their streetscape and homes, in their kitchens and in their recipes and – glorious and golden – poured over the food laid out on their tables.

Torta pasticciotta con le pesche
Custard pie with peaches

The Salento does not have a rich history of sweets. Many have been 'borrowed' from their Sicilian and Calabrian neighbours, using almonds which grow so well in most of southern Italy. Pasticciotto is an exception and typical of the town of Lecce, the largest town in the Salento. You will see oval-shaped mini pasticciotti in most bars and cafés, a rich sweet accompaniment to a morning coffee. The thick custard-like pastry cream is often vanilla-scented, and the pastry, though traditionally made with lard, now tends to be buttery and flaky.

In homes in the Salento, you are more likely to find a large pasticciotto pie, often with less traditional but rather lavish additions to the custardy cream like chocolate or preserved cherries. I rather like adding preserved peaches to mine, but feel free to use other varieties of preserved or even fresh fruit. The pastry cream is lifted by a hint of lemon but you can easily use a scraped vanilla bean instead. I also add significantly less sugar than most; if you have a particularly sweet tooth, increase the quantity in the pastry cream to 150 g (5½ oz). If you are new to making pastry cream or custard, make sure you give it your undivided attention as you do not want to cook the eggs to the point of scrambling.

I admit the pasticciotto pie takes some effort to make, but it is richly rewarding and will last for days. Just make sure you start the recipe a day ahead as the cream filling needs to cool completely overnight.

You will need to start this recipe one day ahead

300 g (10½ oz) tinned peaches (or use fresh if they are in season), drained and cut into narrow segments

1 egg yolk, lightly beaten

icing (confectioners') sugar, for dusting

Pastry cream

750 ml (25½ fl oz/3 cups) milk

peel of ½ lemon, white pith removed

6 egg yolks

110 g (3¾ oz/½ cup) caster (superfine) sugar

110 g (3¾ oz/¾ cup) cornflour (cornstarch), sifted

Pastry

375 g (13 oz/2½ cups) plain (all-purpose) flour

150 g (5½ oz) caster (superfine) sugar

pinch of salt

150 g (5½ oz) chilled unsalted butter, cut into small cubes

1 egg

1 egg white

To make the pastry cream, place the milk and lemon peel in a medium–large saucepan over medium–low heat and gently bring to just below boiling point. Meanwhile, place the egg yolks, sugar and cornflour in a large heatproof bowl and whisk until creamy. When the milk is almost boiling, remove it from the heat. Pour 3 tablespoons of hot milk into the egg mixture and stir vigorously with a wooden spoon. Pour in another 3 tablespoons of milk, mixing the whole time. (If you add too much hot milk at the beginning it will scramble the eggs, so take this part slowly.) Stirring constantly, gradually add the rest of the milk, which will have cooled by now so you can pour a bit more generously.

Return the custard to the saucepan and stir with a wooden spoon over low heat until it starts to thicken – this might take 10 minutes or so, but don't stop stirring and scraping the bottom of the pan, smoothing any lumps with the back of the spoon. At this point you can remove the lemon peel with tongs. When the custard is thicker and noticeably more difficult to stir, remove it from the heat and pour it into a heatproof ceramic bowl. If you see a few lumps, pour it into a sieve and push the cream through with a scraper. Place plastic film directly on the surface of the cream (to stop a skin forming) and over the side of the bowl. Cool to room temperature, then chill in the fridge overnight.

To make the pastry, place the flour, sugar and salt in a large bowl and whisk to remove any lumps. Add half the butter and work it in with your fingertips, then add the remaining butter and work it in until the mixture resembles wet sand. If your work space is warm and the butter starts to melt, put the bowl in the fridge or freezer for a few minutes, then continue to work on it. Whisk the egg and egg white together and add to the flour mixture, mixing with a wooden spoon initially and then with your hands to bring the dough together. Briefly knead the dough until smooth, then wrap it in plastic film and rest in the fridge for at least an hour (overnight is fine).

Preheat the oven to 180°C (350°F). Butter and flour a deep 24 cm (9½ in) round cake tin. Remove the pastry from the fridge and cut it into two portions – you need two-thirds of the dough for the base and side, and one-third for the lid. Roll out the larger portion of dough between two sheets of plastic film to a thickness of 5–6 mm (¼ in), to form a circle large enough to line the base and side of the tin. It should hang slightly over the edge as you will need to fold it over the pastry lid later. Carefully lift the pastry into the prepared tin, using your fingers to gently flatten it onto the base and side. Place in the fridge to chill for 15 minutes if the pastry is becoming soft.

Remove the pastry cream from the fridge – it should now be quite firm. Spread half over the pastry, patting it down with the back of a spoon so it is even, then layer on the peach slices. Pour on the remaining pastry cream and smooth the surface. Chill in the fridge or freezer while you roll out the pastry lid.

Roll out the smaller piece of dough to a thickness of 5–6 mm (¼ in), making a circle that just covers the top of the torta. Place the pastry lid on the filling and fold over the pastry from the side of the tin to form a seal. Trim off any excess, then make a number of light incisions across the top of the lid to mark out 10–12 slices. I push my knife through the pastry along the incisions for about 3 mm (⅛ in) closest to the edge of the lid to help any steam escape during baking. Brush the beaten egg yolk over the pie top.

Bake for 1 hour or until the pastry is cooked and golden, then let the pie cool completely before removing it from the tin. Dust with icing sugar before serving. Leftovers will keep, covered, in the fridge for up to 3 days.

SERVES 10–12

Mostaccioli Pugliesi
Chocolate diamond biscuits

One of the pastry shops I visited in Otranto was selling 'mostaccioli', diamond-shaped chocolate-covered biscotti traditionally eaten at Christmas (not to be confused with the tube-shaped pasta of the same name). They are rich and spicy with an ingredient I could not quite put my finger on so I asked the shop assistant; she told me it was vincotto, with a dash of nutmeg and cloves.

'Vincotto' literally means cooked wine and is the sticky sweet syrup derived from reduced grape juice. To balance the sweetness, I add a touch of good-quality balsamic vinegar to the dough, which sounds odd but gives it a well-balanced depth. Taste the dough and add a touch of balsamic at the end if you feel the mix needs it, or just leave it out altogether. If the dough becomes too sticky while you are working it, add a little bit more flour. The chocolate coating tastes richly decadent – a fitting finale to a Christmas lunch or any family celebration.

60 g (2 oz) natural almonds, toasted

peel of 1 small orange, white pith removed

250 g (9 oz/1⅔ cups) 00 or plain (all-purpose) flour, plus extra if needed

90 g (3 oz) caster (superfine) sugar

1 teaspoon baking powder

pinch of salt

½ teaspoon ground cinnamon

¼ teaspoon ground cloves

¼ teaspoon freshly grated nutmeg

30 g (1 oz) unsweetened dark cocoa powder

20 g (¾ oz) dark chocolate (45% cocoa solids), finely chopped

½ teaspoon vanilla essence

80 ml (2½ fl oz/⅓ cup) vincotto

2½ tablespoons extra virgin olive oil

3 tablespoons warm water, plus extra if needed

½–1 teaspoon balsamic vinegar (optional)

Icing

200 g (7 oz) dark chocolate (45% cocoa solids), broken into pieces

few drops of extra virgin olive oil (optional)

Preheat the oven to 180°C (350°F) and line two large baking trays with baking paper.

Process the almonds in a food processor until they are coarsely ground, and set aside.

Place the orange peel in a mini food processor and process until it is finely chopped.

Place the flour, sugar, baking powder, salt, spices and cocoa in a large bowl and give it a good whisk to remove any lumps. Stir in the ground almonds, chopped orange peel and chocolate, then pour in the vanilla essence and vinocotto, followed by the olive oil in a stream, stirring as you go, until the mixture resembles wet sand. Add half the water and stir, then start to bring the mixture together with your hands. Add enough of the remaining water to form a cohesive but still fairly dry dough. Don't add all the water if it isn't needed (or add a bit more if required to reach the right consistency). If it is too wet, add a bit of extra flour. Taste the dough and add the balsamic vinegar if you think it needs it for balance.

Cut the dough in half and it roll out each portion between two sheets of baking paper to a thickness of 3–4 mm (⅛ in). Using a diamond-shaped cookie cutter with approximately 5 cm (2 in) sides, cut out your biscuits. (If you don't have a diamond-shaped cutter, just use a rectangular one. I must admit I improvised and used a square ravioli cutter with a fluted edge, then trimmed each square into a diamond with 5 cm/2 in sides!)

Place the diamonds on the prepared trays, leaving a little space for spreading, and bake for 12–14 minutes until they feel firm but are still quite soft. Depending on the size of your trays, you may have to bake them in batches. Allow to cool completely on the trays.

To make the icing, place the chocolate in a heatproof bowl set over a saucepan of simmering water, making sure the base of the bowl does not touch the water. Let the chocolate melt, stirring occasionally. I like to add a few drops of olive oil to the chocolate to help the consistency, but this is not essential. Turn off the heat and leave the bowl over the pan.

Line two or three large trays or plates with baking paper.

Working in batches, drop the diamonds into the molten chocolate, using two forks to flip them over and coat on both sides. Lift them from the bowl, allowing the excess chocolate to drip off, and place carefully on the baking paper. Alternatively, only dip half the diamonds in the chocolate if you prefer a lighter biscuit. Allow the chocolate to set before removing the biscuits from the trays or plates. They will keep in an airtight container for a week.

MAKES 35–45

Torta di mandorle al limone
Flourless almond lemon cake

This light, gluten-free cake can be loosely attributed to zia Liliana, aunt of Signora Enrica from Otranto. Enrica told me they make it when the extended family gathers at her house in the historic town. While I love the original, I have changed the recipe a bit, adding more lemon to give it a real tangy hit. I can just imagine eating it on the terrace of the house where I stayed in Otranto, watching the neighbours playing cards in the sunshine and hearing the sea lapping on the shore in the distance.

300 g (10½ oz/2½ cups) almond meal

1 teaspoon baking powder

6 eggs, separated

200 g (7 oz) caster (superfine) sugar

finely grated zest of 2 lemons

80 ml (2½ fl oz/⅓ cup) milk

1 teaspoon vanilla essence

80 ml (2½ fl oz/⅓ cup) freshly squeezed lemon juice

pinch of salt

icing (confectioners') sugar, for dusting

Preheat the oven to 180°C (350°F). Line the base and side of a 28 cm (11 in) springform tin.

Place the almond meal and baking powder in a bowl and whisk briefly to combine and remove any lumps.

Place the egg yolks and caster sugar in the bowl of an electric mixer fitted with the paddle or whisk attachment and beat for several minutes until the mixture becomes pale and light. Add the lemon zest, milk, vanilla, lemon juice and salt and beat until combined, then add the almond meal mixture and beat until incorporated.

Place the egg whites in a clean bowl and whisk until medium–firm peaks form. Working in batches, gently fold the whites into the batter with a spatula, folding from bottom to top so you don't lose aeration. Make sure the batter is well combined, but don't overmix it.

Carefully pour the batter into the prepared tin and bake for 35–40 minutes until the top of the cake is golden and a skewer inserted in the middle comes out clean. Allow to cool in the tin for a few minutes before turning out onto a wire rack to cool completely.

Dust the cake with icing sugar and serve at room temperature with a cup of tea or coffee. The cake will keep in an airtight container for a couple of days.

SERVES 8–10

2

IL GARGANO

Whenever my friend Joe returns home to the Gargano, his first stop after landing is the Caseificio dei Pini, a family-run cheese producer and shop in Siponto, just south of Manfredonia. He orders a mozzarella di bufala on a 'paposcia' (a local type of focaccia bread) and savours every bite. The cheese is creamy and white, and the whey that has been trapped between the stretched layers of mozzarella oozes onto the paposcia. It is only once he has tasted this that Joe feels he is really home in his beloved Gargano.

If you picture the peninsula of Italy as a boot, then the Gargano is the spur just above the heel in the northern part of Puglia. The A14 autostrada bypasses the Gargano, so few tourists have discovered it. Traveling from the south, take a sharp right from the A14 onto the SS89 at Foggia, drive past fields of olive trees for about as long as it takes Joe to eat his paposcia (not long), then through the trees and between the hills you will glimpse the turquoise water of the Adriatic just south of Manfredonia.

Ancient forest covers much of the mountainous promontory, which is now a national park, and in days past it was nearly impossible for travellers to approach by land. The seaside towns of Vieste and Rodi have wide sandy beaches, dotted with candy-striped umbrellas during summer; and from the hilltop town of Peschici, after a steep climb down to the port, you can catch a boat to the Tremiti islands, where legend has it that the Homeric hero Diomedes was buried after the destruction of Troy.

Simple, rustic cooking is at the heart of the Gargano, and olives, cheeses and citrus fruits abound. These ingredients and hundreds more are for sale at Manfredonia's weekly market, where they are watched over by sharp-eyed (and often sharp-tongued) vendors with stupendous powers of mental arithmetic and a legion of recipes to share, if only you will ask. One such vendor was sitting and eating liberal amounts of the spear-leafed peppery 'rucola del Gargano' (local rocket or arugula) and proudly held out a handful for me to try. The leaves were delicious, as were the orange segments from the sweet, pale Biondo variety, their scent filling the air in the spring sunshine.

Manfredonia – or rather the area slightly to the south, Siponto – was an important port in Greek and Roman times. Its name is thought to derive from the word 'seppie', which means cuttlefish, because of the abundant catch by fishermen in those days long past. Seafood has maintained its important place on coastal Gargano dining tables, and the vibrant market at Manfredonia has a bounty of fresh seafood: squid, calamari, sea bass, bream, scallops, snapper and mackerel.

But it is vegetables that dominate the traditional cuisine of the Gargano, especially bitter leafy greens, tomatoes, potatoes, capsicums (bell peppers) and beans (particularly broad/fava beans). Grains and bread also play an important role, being cheap and plentiful fuel for farmers and their families. Old bread was never thrown away; there was always a use for it, even if was simply topped with cooked vegetables and anchovies and drizzled with golden local olive oil.

Similar to the Salento, it is common to find the 'tiella', a baked one-pot dish, traditionally cooked over the hearth. If you live by the coast, you might find a tiella with layers of bitter greens, small fish such as sardines, day-old bread, pecorino, garlic and flat-leaf parsley, drizzled with olive oil and baked. But in the Gargano's rural centre, with its dry-stone walls and flocks of sheep wearing bells that can be heard ringing over the ancient folded landscape of the plateau, fish is a rarity. So a typical meal consists of vegetables, legumes, pasta, bread and, on special occasions, lamb.

A variety of pasta commonly eaten in the Gargano is 'troccoli', a type of spaghetti that is square in cross-section and made with a 'troccolo', a grooved wooden rolling pin that cuts the spaghetti as you roll. The result is similar to what you would get using a 'chitarra', which is a guitar-shaped stringed pasta-cutting device found further north in the region of Abruzzo. Orecchiette is the mainstay of all of Puglia, both the Salento and the Gargano. It is a hearty 'cucina povera' type of pasta, made with just semolina flour and water instead of fine white flour and eggs.

But back to Joe, of paposcia fame. He insisted that I try some of the local Gargano cheeses as well as the buffalo mozzarella – particularly 'caciocavallo podolico', made with the milk of a particular old breed of large-horned cow with a silver-grey coat. The podolico cows graze on the promontory and produce only a small amount of milk, which is used to make table cheese by stretching the curds. When it appears in the markets, the cheese has a fat pear-like body and a little head, with a rope tied around its neck for hanging. I managed to find some at a street market in the town of Peschici. A young man was selling it out of the back of his car – hand-made, unlabelled, cash trade only – and it had been matured for about 4 months. It was as good as Joe promised it would be, particularly with a glass of the local red, Nero di Troia.

Sweets are reserved for special occasions, and are often made with almonds, cooked grape must and citrus fruits. Many believe that in the fifth century Saint Michael appeared several times in Monte Sant'Angelo, high on the southern slopes of the Gargano promontory. The sanctuary, churches and significant tombs in the town are a regular stop on pilgrimages, and when there, devotees might try a typical sweet: 'ostie chiene' (or 'ostie ripiene'), wafer-thin hosts that are used during religious services, filled with delightful caramelised almonds and honey.

Fave fritte
Fried broad beans

One of the gifts that Maria Antonietta gave me when I left her broad (fava) bean farm on the Gargano promontory was a packet of fried broad beans. I asked her whether they were traditional – she admitted that they weren't, but she was producing lots of them as they were so popular. I opened the packet on the drive back to my accommodation, and they were salty and crunchy, an easy rival to the potato chip. As I munched on, I could imagine eating them in the evening before dinner, with an aperitivo or a beer. When I arrived I sheepishly offered my husband the few that remained, as I had eaten the rest.

You will need to start this recipe about 3 hours ahead as the beans need to be soaked before using. Feel free to double or triple the recipe if needed, and have a chilled drink on hand for when the beans are ready.

180 g (6½ oz/1 cup) split or double-podded dried broad (fava) beans

sunflower oil, for deep-frying

sea salt

Wash the dried beans under cold running water and place them in a medium ceramic or glass bowl. Fill the bowl with water so the beans are covered by 3–4 cm (1¼–1½ in). Set aside to let the beans rehydrate.

After about 2 hours, check the beans by trying to break one – it should break quite easily. I also taste the corner of one to see if it can be chewed. If they are not quite ready, leave them for a bit longer and check again. Drain and pat dry with paper towel.

Pour about 500 ml (17 fl oz/2 cups) of sunflower oil into a smallish saucepan and heat to about 170°C (340°F). Test the temperature by carefully dropping in a few beans – if they sizzle and start to fry the oil is ready. Add the beans in batches (depending on the size of your pan) and cook for 3–4 minutes, until they start to brown, stirring regularly with a slotted spoon so they don't sink to the bottom and burn. Remove with the spoon and drain on a plate lined with paper towel. Toss with plenty of sea salt and serve warm or at room temperature.

Fried broad beans will keep in an airtight container for a couple of days, but I guarantee you will eat them all in one sitting.

SERVES 2–4 AS AN ACCOMPANIMENT TO AN APERITIVO

BROAD BEANS
LA CARNE DEI POVERI

Broad beans (or fava beans) have been called 'la carne dei poveri' (the meat of the poor)
and on the northern shores of the Gargano Promontory, around the town of Carpino, you can
find a particular, rather small type called 'la fava di Carpino'. It is smaller than most broad beans,
with plants growing to knee-height and the pods forming around the base of the plant. It is used
as a dried legume rather than fresh.

Maria Antonietta and her husband Michele run a farm that is part of the Slow Food Presidium for the Carpino broad bean. When I met Maria Antonietta at her property in Carpino, she showed me some old photos of her family taken in early summer during the annual broad bean harvest, when the pods start to turn black and dry out. The plant is cut at its base, beans and all, with a scythe and then tied in bundles called 'manocchi'. These are left in the sun to dry completely, and in mid summer the traditional 'pesatura' is carried out. A section of land is prepared by wetting it and laying out a carpet of hay. The bundles of dried beans are then thrown onto the prepared land, and traditionally a horse would trample on them, crushing everything except for the hardened dry bean. These days, a tractor is used (not as romantic, but to the same effect). The next phase is carried out in the afternoon, when there is a breeze. Using a type of wooden broom, the dried-out remnants of the plant are swept into the air and carried off by breeze, leaving the relatively heavier dried broad beans to fall to earth.

Broad beans have been grown in the Gargano for hundreds of years; farmers rotated the crop with wheat or oats. Traditionally buyers from Bari, to the south of the Gargano, would come to Carpino in search of the perfect bean to sell to their customers: the one with the thinnest skin. Growers would assemble stalls in the street and cook their dried beans in the traditional 'pignatta', a tall ceramic vessel with two rear handles that allow the contents to be held and stirred by a flip of the vessel. After being soaked overnight, the beans were cooked simply and slowly in water for several hours until soft. Buyers would taste the cooked beans, determining which they would purchase to take back to Bari.

In the 1950s, production of the fava di Carpino all but ceased as the buyers from Bari were sourcing their beans from elsewhere – industrial processing methods made the product much cheaper than the traditional method employed in the Gargano. Luckily, some older people in the community (including Michele's father) had stored some dried beans, which were planted to start the new generation of broad bean plants. The buyers from Bari no longer arrive to judge their wares, but the quality of the produce speaks for itself. During my visit, Maria Antonietta prepared a plate of 'fave e cicoria' (beans and chicory), the most typical way of eating Carpino broad beans. She doused the dish with her own organic Cannarozzi extra virgin olive oil, lifting a simple nutritious meal to something that was rich, earthy and frankly delicious.

Fave e cicoria
Broad bean stew and chicory

Simple dishes can often be the most satisfying, and this is certainly one of those. Fave e cicoria has become a staple in our household since Maria Antonietta made the dish for me at her broad (fava) bean farm. I can only find split dried broad beans in Australia, so the cooking time is a bit shorter than it would be for double-podded broad beans. If you don't like bitter greens use milder-flavoured silverbeet instead. Just make sure you drizzle the lot with the best olive oil you can afford.

400 g (14 oz) split or double-podded dried broad beans

200 g (7 oz) potatoes, peeled and chopped

sea salt and freshly ground black pepper

350 g (12 oz) leaf chicory

excellent-quality extra virgin olive oil (ideally from Puglia), for drizzling

crusty or day-old bread, to serve

Place the beans in a large ceramic or glass bowl, cover generously with water and soak for about 4 hours (overnight is fine), changing the water a few times. The beans will swell and absorb much of the water.

Drain the beans and place in a large saucepan. Add 500 ml (17 fl oz/2 cups) of water and bring to the boil, then reduce to a simmer, scooping off the froth that forms on the surface (this will subside after a few minutes). Add the potato, then cover and cook over very low heat for 1–2 hours, stirring occasionally and topping up the water as needed. The beans and potatoes will eventually cook through and fall apart – stirring them well towards the end of cooking will help them disintegrate and become creamy. You could also use a stick blender but it is not necessary. The final consistency is all a matter of taste; many opt for a purée but I like it to be more of a thick soup. So add as much water as you think it needs, then season to taste with salt and pepper.

Wash the chicory well and cut off any damaged leaves or thick stalks. Bring a large saucepan of salted water to the boil, drop in the leaves and cook for 3–4 minutes until tender. Drain and set aside to cool, then roughly chop.

Serve on warmed plates. Typically the beans are placed side-by side with the warmed chicory, but I like to put the chicory on top and stir it through the soup. Drizzle liberally with extra virgin olive oil and serve with plenty of bread.

SERVES 4

Sgombri in aceto
Marinated mackerel

Fresh mackerel are beautiful fish to look at, with their large eyes and colourful silvery skin. They are plentiful and easily caught in spring, when they approach the shore to eat tiny anchovies.

You might think that marinating the poached fillets in vinegar would make the flavour overwhelmingly acidic, but it's quite the opposite. It removes any excessive fishiness from the delicate fillets and – when dressed with extra virgin olive oil, garlic and mint – imparts a well-balanced lightness. It is the kind of appetiser you would want to share on the terrace with close friends on a warm summer night over a bottle of crisp Fiano, a white wine typical of the Gargano.

I usually ask my fishmonger to clean the innards from the mackerel, and then fillet them at home, although you could always see if your fishmonger would do the filleting part too. Make sure you remove any bones with fine tweezers – there aren't many but it's worth taking the trouble. If you can't find mackerel, use large sardine fillets instead.

300 g (10½ oz) mackerel fillets (about 900 g/2 lb before cleaning)

250–500 ml (8½–17 fl oz/ 1–2 cups) white wine vinegar

2 tablespoons finely chopped mint

1 large clove garlic, finely chopped

3 tablespoons good-quality extra virgin olive oil

sea salt

Wrap the mackerel fillets in a clean piece of fine white cloth (I use pieces of old cotton sheets but you could also use muslin or a tea towel) and tie the ends with string or elastic bands, so it looks like a bon-bon. Place the parcel in a saucepan filled with room-temperature water and bring to the boil. Reduce the heat and simmer gently for about 2 minutes, then remove the parcel and allow most of the water to drip off it.

Place the parcel of mackerel in a medium ceramic or glass bowl and pour in enough vinegar to cover the fish completely. Set aside for 1 hour.

Combine the mint, garlic and olive oil in a bowl and set aside to steep.

After an hour, remove the parcel from the vinegar and open the ends. Gently remove the fish fillets (take care as they may stick to the cloth and break). They should be mostly white; if they are still very pink, drop them directly into the vinegar and check them in 5–10 minutes. It's fine if they are pale pink.

Pat the fish dry with paper towel and place on a serving plate. Drizzle with the infused olive oil and season to taste with sea salt.

SERVES 4 AS AN APPETISER

Polpettone di melanzane con salsa di pomodoro e basilico
Eggplant log with tomato and basil sauce

In the Gargano, eggplants (aubergines) are mainly stuffed and baked. My friend Angela, whose family is from Peschici, tells me that when she was growing up her mother used to make eggplant 'polpette' (meatballs, without the meat) with black olives and capers. They were pan-fried and topped with a simple sauce of tomato and basil – delicious. Rather than making them into individual balls, I like to shape the eggplant mix into a 'polpettone' (a loaf or log), adding a good handful of sharp pecorino and a big pinch of aromatic oregano. The log is sliced, topped with a tomato and basil sauce and served on a platter, making a festive vegetarian main meal. It will remain moist for days, and is just as tasty warm as it is at room temperature.

3 medium–large (about 1 kg/ 2 lb 3 oz) eggplants (aubergines)

1 zucchini (courgette)

1 clove garlic, crushed

50 g (1¾ oz) pecorino, grated

1 tablespoon salted capers, soaked in water for 10 minutes, drained

about 7 dried black olives, pitted and roughly chopped

100 g (3½ oz) crustless fresh bread, torn into medium crumbs

1 teaspoon dried oregano

2 eggs, lightly beaten

sea salt and freshly ground black pepper

3–4 tablespoons dried breadcrumbs (optional)

basil leaves, to serve

Sauce

2 tablespoons extra virgin olive oil

1 clove garlic, thickly sliced

1 x 400 g (14 oz) tin whole peeled tomatoes

1–2 sprigs basil

sea salt and freshly ground black pepper

Preheat the oven to 180°C (350°F) and line a baking tray with baking paper.

Wash the eggplants, then cut them in half lengthways. Score the cut surface in a criss-cross pattern then place, cut-side down, on the prepared tray. Bake for 30 minutes or until the flesh is soft, then remove and allow to cool slightly (leave the oven on). Scoop out the contents with a large spoon, discarding the skin. Place the eggplant flesh in an old clean tea towel and wring to remove the excess liquid (there will be quite a lot). Discard the liquid.

Roughly chop the eggplant flesh if it hasn't already broken into chunks and place in a large bowl. Wash and trim the zucchini, then grate into the bowl using the coarse side of a box grater. Add the garlic, pecorino, capers, olives, fresh breadcrumbs, oregano and egg, and salt and pepper to taste. Check the consistency of the mixture; if it is too wet, add as many dried breadcrumbs as you need to bring it together. You should be able to shape it into a rough log.

Line a small loaf tin with baking paper – mine is 21 cm x 11 cm (8¼ in x 4¼ in) and is 6 cm (2½ in) deep.

Place the log the prepared loaf tin and pat it flat with the back of a spoon. Bake for 50 minutes or until cooked through and firm to touch.

Meanwhile, make the sauce, heat the olive oil in a medium saucepan over high heat, then drop in the slices of garlic and let them sizzle until just coloured. Add the tomatoes and cook for a minute or so, then break them apart with a wooden spoon. Reduce the heat to medium, add the basil sprigs and simmer for about 20 minutes. Season to taste with salt and pepper, then remove the garlic slices and basil.

Remove the eggplant log from the oven and allow to cool for about 5 minutes, then gently flip it out of the tin onto a chopping board. Cut it into thick slices and arrange on a serving plate. Top with the tomato sauce and scatter on basil leaves to serve.

SERVES 4 AS A LIGHT LUNCH

Orecchiette con polpa di agnello, pomodorini e rucola
Pasta with lamb, tomatoes and rocket

We spent a day in Monte Sant'Angelo, travelling up a precipitously steep road from our accommodation near Mattinata. It started snowing when we arrived, even though it was late April, and everyone was rushing out of the weather to take shelter. Maybe Saint Michael (who is said to have appeared in the town in the 400s) was looking out for us, as the steps we climbed up seeking shelter lead directly to a restaurant! Called Al Medioevo, it's one of the best places to eat in town, and also one where local ingredients are used to make variations on traditional dishes. For my first course I chose orecchiette, the traditional 'little ear' pasta and a sauce made with lamb, tomatoes and the same peppery rocket that I had tasted at the weekly market in Manfredonia the day before. I loved it, and this simple dish is now a regular in my Australian kitchen.

1 tablespoon extra virgin olive oil, plus extra to serve

½ medium brown or white onion, finely diced

300 g (10½ oz) good-quality minced (ground) lamb

80 ml (2½ fl oz/⅓ cup) dry white wine

300 g (10½ oz) cherry tomatoes, quartered

sea salt

300 g (10½ oz) dried orecchiette

large handful of rocket (arugula) leaves

freshly ground black pepper (optional)

60 g (2 oz) grated aged pecorino, or to taste

Heat the olive oil in a large frying pan over medium–low heat, add the onion and cook gently for about 10 minutes or until softened, translucent and pale gold. Add the lamb and cook, stirring frequently, until the meat is browned all over. Increase the heat to medium–high and add the wine. Let it bubble away and when it starts to reduce, add the tomatoes and reduce the heat to medium–low and continue to simmer as you cook the pasta. Add salt to taste.

Bring a large saucepan of salted water to the boil and cook the orecchiette until al dente, following the instructions on the packet.

Drain the pasta and add it to the sauce, stirring well to coat. Stir in the rocket and season with pepper (if using). Divide the orecchiette among warmed plates, scatter with plenty of pecorino and finish with a good drizzle of extra virgin olive oil.

SERVES 4 AS A STARTER

Troccoli con le seppie
Black spaghetti with cuttlefish

Vieste might be the most remote town on the Gargano promontory but it seems to be one of the most popular, with a buzzing beach scene. We visited early in the tourist season and the only place we could find open for lunch was Il Dragone. It was an extraordinary place, set into a cave, with bare rock walls next to the tables. We were the only people eating there and were quite spoilt, with two waiters to ourselves.

My favourite dish from that day was an inky black pile of square-cut spaghetti and cuttlefish. Traditionally a 'troccolo' would be used to shape the pasta, a kind of wooden rolling pin with protruding wooden prongs that cut the sheet of pasta. As I don't have a troccolo, I used my chitarra (see page 20) to make these at home and the results were pretty similar. A sturdy long-bladed knife would also do the trick, or you could simply use store-bought squid ink pasta. Feel free to use calamari or squid instead of cuttlefish, although I think the latter is the easiest to prepare.

4 cuttlefish (about 900 g/2 lb), cleaned (see page 16)

2–3 tablespoons extra virgin olive oil

1 small brown onion, finely diced

1 clove garlic, crushed

2 anchovy fillets

125 ml (4 fl oz/½ cup) dry white wine

2 teaspoons tomato paste

2 teaspoons squid ink (in a jar or the ink sacs from the cuttlefish)

sea salt and freshly ground black pepper

finely grated lemon zest, to garnish (optional)

Pasta

200 g (7 oz/1⅓ cups) plain (all-purpose) flour, plus extra for dusting

200 g (7 oz) superfine semolina (semola rimacinata)

2 eggs

2 teaspoons squid ink (in a jar or the ink sacs from the cuttlefish)

Open up each cuttlefish body so that it is a flat triangle on a chopping board and cut it into narrow strips (approximately the same width as the spaghetti). Cut from the top of the hood down to the base so it doesn't curl as it cooks.

Heat the olive oil in a medium frying pan over low heat, add the onion and cook for 15 minutes or until very soft and starting to colour. Add the garlic and anchovies and cook, breaking up the anchovies, for 1–2 minutes until fragrant. Increase the heat to medium–high, add the cuttlefish and cook for 5 minutes, stirring frequently, until the liquid from the cuttlefish evaporates. Pour in the wine, then reduce the heat and simmer, covered, for 20 minutes, stirring occasionally. Stir in the tomato paste and squid ink and cook, covered, for a further 30 minutes or until the cuttlefish is fork tender (don't be afraid to cook it for longer if it is still tough). Season to taste with salt and pepper.

While the cuttlefish is cooking, follow the instructions on pages 22–23 for making egg pasta, dropping in the squid ink as you combine the flours, eggs and about 100 ml (3½ fl oz) water. Cover and allow to rest for at least 30 minutes.

After the dough has rested, cut it into quarters. Working with one portion at a time, roll it out on a surface that has been lightly dusted with superfine semolina. You can use a pasta machine or rolling pin to roll it to a 2 mm (1/16 in) thickness. Cut it into square spaghetti with a grooved wooden 'troccolo' (or use a chitarra or cut it by hand). Dust the prepared pasta with superfine semolina and cover with a clean tea towel to prevent it from drying out. Repeat with the remaining dough.

Bring a large saucepan of salted water to the boil. Drop in the pasta and cook until al dente (the time will vary, depending on the thickness of the pasta). Drain, reserving a little of the pasta water in a cup. Toss the pasta through the sauce, adding some of the reserved cooking water if it looks a bit dry.

Divide the pasta among warmed plates, finish with a scattering of lemon zest (if using) and serve immediately.

SERVES 4

Tiella cozze, riso e patate
Mussel, rice and potato bake

Rice, potatoes and salty mussels are layered in this traditional one-pot dish. Said to be from Bari, I have eaten it in both Lecce and Manfredonia, and according to popular opinion, the use of rice in the dish harks back to the Spanish invasion of Puglia. So it has a bit of everywhere in it! The rice needs to be cooked until it is fluffy with only a hint of bite, so make sure you add plenty of water. Everything tastes better with a bit of cheese, so topping the dish with a good sprinkling of aged pecorino gives a sharp taste as well as a golden topping.

This is particularly nice accompanied by a glass of white Fiano from the Gargano.

1 clove garlic, finely chopped or minced

3 tablespoons white wine

700 g (1 lb 9 oz) fresh mussels, cleaned and debearded (see page 17)

1 tablespoon extra virgin olive oil

600 g (1 lb 5 oz) potatoes, peeled and cut into 4–5 mm (¼ in) thick slices

1 small white onion, thinly sliced

500 g (1 lb 2 oz) ripe cherry tomatoes (or other small tomatoes), quartered,

3 tablespoons finely chopped flat-leaf parsley leaves

sea salt and freshly ground black pepper

300 g (10½ oz) short-grain rice

50 g (1¾ oz) grated aged pecorino

Preheat the oven to 200°C (400°F).

Place a large frying pan with a lid over medium–high heat. Add the garlic, wine and mussels in a single layer, then cover and cook for about 2 minutes, shaking the pan every 30 seconds or so. Remove the open shells and set aside. Replace the lid and cook the remaining mussels for another 30 seconds, then check again for open shells and remove those that have opened. Repeat a few more times, then discard any unopened shells after 5 minutes.

Strain the liquid left in the pan and reserve. Using a small sharp knife, separate the mussel meat from the open shells at the base of the stalk.

Drizzle the olive oil over the base of a 24 cm (9½ in) round baking dish (ideally terracotta) and top with one-third of the potato slices. Next add half the onion, half the tomatoes, 1 tablespoon of parsley, a pinch of salt and some pepper, half the rice, then half the mussels, making sure the opening of the mussel flesh is facing up. Then add half the remaining potatoes and repeat the layers described above, finishing with a final layer of potato. Pour the reserved mussel liquid into the dish, along with enough hot water to bring the liquid just below the top layer of potatoes.

Scatter on the pecorino, then cover with foil and bake for 45 minutes. Check the potatoes are cooked through. If they are still firm, bake for another 5–10 minutes, then check again. When they are ready, remove the foil and bake for 5–10 minutes until the top is golden. Rest for at least 30 minutes, then scatter over the remaining parsley and serve.

SERVES 6–8

Agnello con patate al forno
Lamb and potato bake

Meat is a rarity in traditional Gargano cooking, but in times of celebration it is often lamb that graces the table. This rustic dish with bite-sized pieces of lamb and potato is a simple Pugliese classic that I love to cook for the family on a Sunday night. A scattering of ripe cherry tomatoes makes it moist and adds a vibrant splash of colour to this modest-looking meal.

In keeping with the rustic theme, I usually put the pan in the centre of the table so everyone can serve themselves.

3 tablespoons extra virgin olive oil

1 kg (2 lb 3 oz) lamb shoulder, cut into bite-sized pieces

2 cloves garlic, skin on, crushed

1 rosemary sprig, plus extra leaves to garnish

125 ml (4 fl oz/½ cup) dry white wine

1 brown onion, thinly sliced

650 g (1 lb 7 oz) potatoes, peeled and cut into chunks

½ teaspoon chilli flakes

sea salt and freshly ground black pepper

250 g (9 oz) cherry tomatoes, halved

Preheat the oven to 180°C (350°F).

Heat the olive oil in a 30 cm (12 in) flameproof baking dish over medium heat. Add the lamb, garlic cloves and rosemary and cook, stirring frequently, until the meat starts to colour. Increase the heat, add the wine and let it bubble away until about half of it has evaporated. Add the onion, reduce the heat and cook for about 8 minutes or until the onion has softened. Add the potato chunks and chilli flakes, season with salt and pepper and stir well to coat. Finally, scatter on the cherry tomatoes. Try to ensure most of the lamb is covered by vegetables, as this will prevent it from drying out too much.

Place in the oven and bake for 1 hour or until the potatoes are nicely roasted. Check occasionally and add a bit of water if the dish is starting to look dry. Remove from the oven, then cover and rest for 5 minutes. There should be quite a bit of tasty liquid in the base of the dish, which is delicious drizzled over the top. Garnish with extra rosemary leaves and serve.

SERVES 6–8

Orata alla brace
Barbecued whole bream

We have a portable grill on our balcony; I ask my husband Mark to get the fire going for outdoor cooking well in advance as it takes a good hour to get to the point where the coals are white hot and no longer smoking. When he has done all the hard work, I emerge from the kitchen wearing my apron, carrying a fish doused in olive oil, lemon, salt and herbs, and often holding a wine glass. The cooking is the easy part, the apron is probably just for show, and the wine is for me to enjoy while I am cooking. It's an arrangement that works very well!

If you cannot find bream, snapper is also delicious cooked over the coals. Just make sure the fish is as fresh as can be.

1 kg (2 lb 3 oz) bream (either 1 large fish or 2–3 small ones)

sea salt and freshly ground black pepper

125 ml (4 fl oz/½ cup) extra virgin olive oil

125 ml (4 fl oz/½ cup) freshly squeezed lemon juice

1 teaspoon dried oregano

1 lemon, sliced

oregano sprigs, to garnish

crisp green salad, to serve

Clean and descale the fish (or ask your fishmonger to do it for you), then wash and pat dry. Rub salt and pepper on the skin as well as a bit in the cavity. Place the olive oil and lemon juice in a large bowl and add the whole fish. Scatter on half the dried oregano, then turn the fish over and scatter over the rest. Marinate for 1 hour, turning the fish occasionally so the marinade is evenly distributed.

Remove the fish from the marinade and arrange the lemon slices over the top. Grill over hot coals (or a preheated barbecue), brushing with the remaining marinade every 5 minutes or so. The exact cooking time will depend on the thickness of the fish in the middle, but as a rough guide three fish will take 20 minutes, two fish about 25 minutes, and one fish 30–35 minutes. Test by checking the flesh near the belly where an incision was made to remove the innards; if the flesh is white and comes away easily from the bones, it is ready.

Garnish the fish with oregano sprigs and serve with a green salad.

SERVES 4

Marmellata di arance dolci
Sweet orange jam

During the 'sagra degli agrumi' (citrus festival) in Rodi, I tasted a thick, sweet orange jam, and I imagine the variety of oranges used must have been very sweet to balance out the bitterness of the rind. I eventually found a recipe by Pellegrino Artusi in his quasi-bible of Italian cooking, La scienza in cucina e l'arte di mangiar bene *(Science in the Kitchen and the Art of Eating Well) which cleverly requires the oranges to be soaked in water for three days to remove the bitterness.*

It worked out beautifully, resulting in a thick jam with pieces of rind still intact but soft, and without a hint of bitterness. Of course it makes an ideal breakfast jam, but because I love the combination of chocolate and orange, I have also paired it with a cocoa crostata (see page 100). Amazing!

You will need to start this recipe three days ahead

1.5 kg (3 lb 5 oz) sweet in-season oranges, preferably organic, pierced all over with a fork

juice of 1 small lemon

about 1.5 kg (3 lb 5 oz) granulated sugar

2 tablespoons white rum

Place the oranges in a large bowl or bucket and cover with water. Cover with a clean tea towel and place in a room that is not heated. Change the water every 12 hours for 3 days. On the fourth day, drain the oranges and remove the rind at the ends of the oranges. Cut each orange in half lengthways, then cut into segments no more than 5 mm (¼ in) thick (you can cut them thinner or into pieces if you do not like chunky jam). Weigh the oranges (I still had 1.5 kg/3 lb 5 oz as they had absorbed some water) and place in a large saucepan that will easily fit them all. Add the same weight of water (in my case, 1.5 litres/52 fl oz) and the lemon juice, then bring to the boil and allow to boil for 10 minutes. Weigh out the same amount of sugar as you had sliced oranges and add this to the pan – it should dissolve fairly quickly. Bring to the boil, then reduce the heat so the orange mixture bubbles away gently.

Check every 15 minutes or so, giving the mixture a good stir. After about 1¾ hours the syrup will start to reduce and thicken.

Meanwhile, preheat the oven to 110°C (225°F). Wash some lidded glass jars so they are completely clean, then place them in the oven with their lids upturned to sterilise them. Turn the oven off after about 30 minutes and leave them there until needed. I also sterilise a 500 ml (17 fl oz/2 cup) heatproof glass jug at this point, as I will need it later to help me pour the jam into jars.

Place a small plate in the freezer.

When the jam mixture has reduced and the syrup is looking thicker, test it for readiness. Place a small teaspoon of jam on the chilled plate. If it sets and is not too runny, it is ready. If it is still runny, return the plate to the freezer and cook the jam mixture for another 5–10 minutes before testing again.

When the jam is ready, remove it from the heat and stir in the rum. Remove the jars from the oven and pour the jam directly into them (or use the sterilised jug to fill the jars) to about 5 mm (¼ in) from the top. Secure the jars with the sterilised lids, them turn them upside-down. Set aside until the next day, then turn them the right way up. This should form a seal, allowing you to keep the jam for up to a year. Once opened, store it in the fridge.

MAKES 5–6 JARS

CITRUS FRUITS
OF THE GARGANO

On what felt like the coldest day of the year I called Signor Lazzaro Russo from the medieval hamlet of Vico – I wanted to arrange a meeting with him to learn more about the citrus fruits of the Gargano peninsula. Maybe he heard my teeth chattering. 'Come and thaw in Rodi on the coast; it is much warmer here and I can show you the "oasi degli agrumi" (the little oasis where we grow citrus trees)', he told me. 'This weekend we are holding a "sagra" (festival)!'

CITRUS FRUIT
OF THE GARGANO

The seaside town of Rodi is only half an hour from Vico, but it felt like a world away as we drove down the mountain, through olive groves and past oak trees, to see the wide sandy beaches and striped blue and yellow beach umbrellas of Rodi in the early spring sunshine.

The oasi is high on a rocky cliff, protected from the winds that rush inland from the Adriatic Sea by a wall of bay and oak trees. The scent of oranges filled the air as I walked along the path that lead through the historic gardens to the old two-storey building that houses the Slow Food Presidium, where I was to meet Lazzaro, the official contact for the citrus producers of the Presidium. The walls of the upper room of the oasi's offices were decorated with colourful posters from the turn of the last century, showing orange and lemon branches, wooden crates of fruit ready to be transported, sturdy men loading crates into ships ready to sail, seaside towns, and smiling women in traditional dress bearing baskets of citrus fruit.

I asked Lazzaro to tell me a bit about the history of the citrus fruits and he introduced me to Giuseppe, who he said knows the story better than anyone. Giuseppe has a lilting and sonorous voice, and a gift for story telling. He explained that 'agrumi' (citrus fruit) have been grown at Rodi, Vico and Ischitella on the Garganic Peninsula since medieval times and, until recently, it was the only place in the Adriatic that grew citrus.

Before the 1500s the fruit was a bitter variety (melangolo or pomo citrino) with little juice. Enter the Portuguese, who introduced the sweeter variety of orange into the Mediterranean, possibly via China or India. Sweet oranges quickly became popular and in the 1600s they made their way to the Gargano.

Underground springs feed the citrus groves and the season in the Gargano is later than in other parts of Italy, with certain varieties producing well into spring, summer and even autumn. We stood among the trees, shaded from the warm sun that drew the fruits' perfume from their skins, and Giuseppe told me the story of Saint Valentine, the patron saint of Vico, and his connection to the oranges grown on the Gargano. The legend says that on his feast day (14 February), whoever drinks the juice of freshly picked oranges will fall in love with whoever gives it to them. Luckily we were there in April so there was no danger of me falling in love with anyone bearing fruit juice!

The posters I'd seen in the offices of the Slow Food Presidium tell the story of a boom in the production of citrus fruits from the mid to late 1800s. Ships criss-crossed the Adriatic, from Rodi to Trieste, Zara and Split, carrying oranges for sale in Austria, Russia and the Balkans, and back again carrying wood from the eastern Adriatic shores. Oranges from the Gargano made their way to the United States, first on boats to the port of Manfredonia, then by train to Naples and finally across the Atlantic. The fruit travelled well, arriving in good shape even after the 40-day journey; the delayed season complemented that of the Sicilian citrus crop, meaning fruit was available fresh for export for most of the year. The town of Rodi in particular experienced a boom. Giuseppe explained that oranges at the time were one lira per kilogram (2 lb 3 oz), and that 15,000 kilograms (about 33,000 pounds) were produced per year, which was a substantial amount of money at the time for those who controlled most of the production, such as the De Felice, Ciampa and Russo families. They attended world fairs to show their produce, winning medals for their citrus fruit in Chicago, Paris and Edinburgh.

However, with every rise there is a fall and the United States started producing its own crop. The loss of trade had a significant effect on the Gargano citrus fruit business. World unrest at the turn of the century and the world wars in the 20th century would have destroyed the Gargano's citrus production if it weren't for a small, passionate group of producers in Rodi, Vico and Ischitella. They continue to grow the traditional citrus varieties for which the Gargano earned its renown: Duretta and Bionda oranges and Femminello lemons, plus a number of newer cross-breeds. And more recently, there was the international recognition that came from the formation of a Slow Food Presidium, a vital milestone to ensure the continuation of production and preserve the story of citrus fruits of the Gargano.

The oasi itself contains a small number of different varieties, scattered through the historic gardens. On the day I visited, Giuseppe was helping clean up the grounds, ready for a cooking demonstration for a large school group that would be held as part of the festival the following weekend.

That weekend we tried the different varieties of oranges, pairing them with hand-made pasta, bread and sweet pastry. We had salads made with thin slices of orange and lemon, dressed with local olive oil; we ate olives marinated with wedges of lemon, and tried sweet orange jam. In the nearby town piazza, teenagers were dressed in red, yellow, green and black traditional costumes, performing for the crowds in celebration of the agrumi, which are still a great source of pride for the people of Rodi.

Crostata di cacao con marmellata di arance
Chocolate and orange crostata

Sweet orange jam brings the citrus flavour and scent of the Gargano back to me in this cocoa crostata. I ate a similar one in Vieste at Il Dragone, a memorable restaurant set into a cave. The crostata base was thick and chocolatey, and liberally covered with sweet orange jam.

You can use your own sweet orange jam (page 94) or look for a store-bought jam in a speciality store. I would advise against using bitter marmalade as it will give the crostata quite a different flavour; opt for apricot jam instead, as it pairs very well with the cocoa.

You will need to start this recipe one day ahead

320 g (11¼ oz) plain (all-purpose) flour

100 g (3½ oz) caster (superfine) sugar

50 g (1¾ oz/½ cup) unsweetened dark cocoa powder

2 scant teaspoons baking powder

pinch of salt

150 g (5½ oz) chilled butter, cut into small cubes

2 eggs, lightly beaten

2 tablespoons milk

300 g (10½ oz) Sweet orange jam (page 94)

icing (confectioners') sugar, for dusting (optional)

mascarpone, to serve (optional)

Place the flour, sugar, cocoa, baking powder and salt in the bowl of an electric mixer fitted with the paddle attachment and whisk briefly to combine and remove any lumps. Add the butter and process until the mixture is crumbly, then add the egg and milk and mix on low speed until it forms a stiff cohesive dough. Do not overmix. Gently form into a ball, wrap in plastic film and allow to rest in the fridge overnight.

Preheat the oven to 180°C (350°F) and line a 25 cm (10 in) tart tin with a removable base.

Remove the pastry from the fridge and cut into two portions – you need two-thirds of the dough for the base and side, and one-third for the lattice top. The dough should be easy to roll out once it warms up slightly. Roll out the larger portion of dough between two sheets of plastic film to a thickness of 3–4 mm (⅛ in), to form a circle large enough to line the base and side of the tin. Carefully lift the pastry into the prepared tin, using your fingers to gently flatten it onto the base and side, cutting off the excess with a sharp knife.

Spoon the jam on top. Place the tart in the fridge while you roll out the remaining dough to a thickness of 3–4 mm (⅛ in). Cut the dough into strips (mine were just under 1 cm/½ in wide), then arrange the strips in a lattice over the jam, gently pinching the ends to attach them to the pastry rim.

Bake for 40–50 minutes until the pastry is golden and cooked through. Allow to cool for a few minutes, then carefully remove the crostata from the tin and dust with icing sugar (if using) while it is still warm. Eat at room temperature, with or without a dollop of mascarpone on the side. This crostata is even nicer the next day.

SERVES 10–12

Salame dolce ai sapori degli agrumi del Gargano
Spiral biscotti with citrus fruits

I met Gargano-born Gianni di Blase at one of the events the Oasi degli Agrumi (Citrus Oasis) was running for their 'sagra' (festival) in Rodi. He was teaching a group of teenagers to make pastry outdoors, not an easy task on what turned out to be a rather warm day. The sun was shining, the children were running amok and the pastry was becoming very soft. Gianni (now a pastry chef living in northern Italy) was patient and gentle with them, letting everyone have a turn at rolling and cutting the dough, in spite of the fact that it was softening at an alarming rate.

One of the treats he made that day was a sweet 'salame', a type of biscuit or cookie, where the pastry is rolled into a salami shape, then cut into rounds and baked. As we were celebrating the local citrus fruit, I suggested that Gianni could grate some citrus zest onto the dough before rolling it out – orange for the chocolate part and lemon for the plain pastry. 'Che buon idea', he told the children, 'non si finisce mai di imparare nella vita.' ('What a good idea, you never stop learning in life.') He christened the resultant spiral biscotti 'salame dolce ai sapori del Gargano'.

Lemon pastry

335 g (11¾ oz/2¼ cups) plain
(all-purpose) flour

135 g (4¾ oz) caster (superfine)
sugar

2 teaspoons baking powder

pinch of salt

175 g (6 oz) chilled butter,
cut into small cubes

finely grated zest of ½ lemon

1 egg, lightly beaten

Chocolate and orange pastry

300 g (10½ oz/2 cups) plain
(all-purpose) flour

135 g (4¾ oz) caster (superfine)
sugar

2 teaspoons baking powder

20 g (¾ oz) unsweetened dark
cocoa powder

pinch of salt

175 g (6 oz) chilled butter,
cut into small cubes

finely grated zest of 1 orange

1 egg, lightly beaten

The method for making the dough is the same for both flavours. Place all the dry ingredients in a large bowl and lightly whisk to combine. Add the butter and rub into the dry ingredients with your fingertips until the mixture is crumbly and resembles wet sand. Scatter on the citrus zest, then mix in the egg and gently bring the pastry together into a ball. (You could also use a food processer to do this, if preferred.) Wrap the dough balls separately in plastic film and place in the fridge overnight.

Remove the chocolate and orange pastry from the fridge and cut it in half. Wrap one half in plastic film and return it to the fridge. Roll out the remaining portion between two sheets of plastic film to a 24 cm (9½ in) square. I use two sheets of plastic film to help me roll out the pastry – one under the pastry and one over the top. I lift it up frequently as I am rolling to prevent the film from tearing, and also flip it onto the other side. However, feel free to use a floured work surface instead of plastic film, if you prefer.

Repeat with the lemon pastry.

Place the rolled-out chocolate and orange pastry directly on the rolled-out lemon pastry and, using the plastic film (if using), roll it up into a salami shape, trimming the ends to make it even. Wrap the roll in plastic film and place it in the fridge for at least 30 minutes to chill.

Now repeat with the remaining balls of pastry in the fridge to make a second salami shape and chill for 30 minutes.

Preheat the oven to 180°C (350°F) and line two large baking trays with baking paper.

Take one chilled salami out of the fridge and remove the plastic film. Using a sharp knife, cut it into 3–4 mm (⅛ in) thick rounds and place on the prepared trays, leaving plenty of room for spreading. Repeat with the remaining salami. Bake for 10 minutes or until cooked through and the lemony pastry is pale golden. Cool on the trays for a few minutes, then transfer to a wire rack to cool completely. The biscuits will keep in an airtight container for a week or so.

MAKES ABOUT 70

3

LA COSTA DEI TRABOCCHI

The landscape changed as we drove north from the Gargano towards Abruzzo: the land was a deeper green, more exuberant, a mosaic of vines, olives and conifers. Farms with extensive pastures curved down towards the sea, and the snow-capped peaks of Gran Sasso formed a stunning backdrop. There was an occasional glimpse of the Adriatic and of spindly wooden fishing constructions on stilts called 'trabocchi'.

We stayed in Manoppello at my friend Giulia's B&B and farm, which is typical of the area just inland from the coast, where small farms line hillsides lush with vines and almond trees, and the occasional cluster of stone houses and church spires can be seen in the distance.

Giulia has a passion for local and traditional food and at her table we shared meals of freshly picked baby broad (fava) beans served whole and ready to peel, local sheep's milk cheese (pecorino), homemade garlicky liver sausages, pasta made with spelt or farro from the Majella mountains, and carafes of her father-in-law's homemade Montepulciano wine.

She took us to coastal Ortona to visit her friend Fausto's family-run 'agriturismo', a working farm with a restaurant and accommodation called L'Antico Feudo. Acres of vines surround the agriturismo, which has views to the coast. Every Friday night there is a feast of home-grown organic chickens roasted over the open fire, served with braised greens called 'foglie' (literally meaning 'leaves') and 'pizza di granoturco', a type of poor man's bread made with polenta flour or cornmeal and cooked under the hot coals.

In addition to cornmeal, wheat and maize play an important role in the traditional foods of this area. In the hills they grow farro (spelt), which is used to make bread and pasta. Stoneground farro is mixed with cornmeal or even used on its own to make a nutty polenta. Square-cut spaghetti is made using a rolling pin and wooden frame with metal strings called a 'chitarra' (guitar). Chickpeas grow readily and are eaten often; a typical dish is chickpeas served with wholegrain pasta in a soupy broth. Meat – especially lamb and rabbit – is eaten at celebrations, where it is cooked with garlic and herbs over hot coals.

A feature of the coast between Ortona and Vasto are the trabocchi themselves, popular with the locals for weekend walks. A disused railway line runs parallel to the beach and we took a long walk along the rocky line, past the many trabocchi. Acacia trees were in full bloom with their tiny grape-like bunches of flowers, making the air smell like honey. The trabocchi have been there as long as anyone can remember, and it is believed that the first trabocchieri (trabocchi operators) were farmers, not fishermen. The construction of the trabocchi on promontories of coastal land was an important connection between land and sea, a way of accessing the bounty of the sea without venturing into a boat. The trabocchieri's purpose was survival: to catch food to supplement the produce from the land. Nets were lowered from the trabocco to reach deeper waters where various types of seafood were plentiful, particularly squid, cuttlefish, sardines and mackerel. The food prepared by the families of the trabocchieri was often a marriage of vegetables and smaller seafood: squid and greens, sardines and potatoes, along with the reliable staples of bread and pasta.

Dried sweet chilli peppers tied on long strings hang in many kitchens and terraces in the area. They are not only decorative, but are used in countless dishes. Whenever I asked a cook or stallholder how they would use a particular meat or vegetable, most recipes included a few of those dried peppers. In a typical seafood stew (brodetto) from Pescara, a dried pepper is added to the cooking oil and left to infuse, then removed, chopped and scattered over the finished dish.

Traditional sweets often contain local almonds and are flavoured with aniseed liqueur. For breakfast Giulia often made 'pizzelle', crisp thin sweet waffles made with a lacy-patterned iron traditionally held over the hearth. We ate them with homemade preserves of grapes and cherries, and plenty of good strong coffee.

Fagioli e alici
Borlotti beans and anchovies

Borlotti beans were a constant in my father's vegetable garden. We would harvest them when the pods were plump and streaked with vanilla and pink, and then sit in the kitchen podding them while listening to the radio (my mother always had it on a station that played old-time singers like Perry Como). We would eat the beans stewed until tender, and we'd also dry them for use through the year, then use the same batch for the next year's crop.

If you tend to use tinned beans rather than dried, it is easier than you think to make the switch. Put dried beans in a bowl of water before you go to bed and leave them to soak overnight. In the morning they will be nice and plump, ready to be rinsed, drained and cooked. The cooked beans make a substantial addition to any dish and are used all over Italy, although they are rather plain on their own. Dressing them up with anchovies, garlic and dried sweet peppers gives them a delightful spicy saltiness.

You can use anchovies in oil or salt for this recipe – just remember to clean any fine bones that are still attached to the fillet. If you are using salted anchovies, rinse them well and pat them dry before use.

200 g (7 oz) dried borlotti beans, soaked overnight (or 250 g/9 oz tinned borlotti beans)

2–3 tablespoons extra virgin olive oil

1–2 dried sweet chilli peppers (or use hot ones with the seeds removed)

1 clove garlic, crushed

6 anchovy fillets

2 teaspoons finely chopped flat-leaf parsley

Drain the borlotti beans, then place in a saucepan of salted water and boil for about 30 minutes or until they are tender but still retain their shape. Drain and set aside.

Heat 2 tablespoons of olive oil in a small frying pan over low heat, add the dried peppers and cook until they start to soften and infuse the oil. Remove the peppers and allow to cool, then chop them finely, removing the seeds. Add the garlic to the infused oil (adding another splash of oil if needed) and cook until fragrant. Add the anchovies and cook for a few minutes, breaking them up with a wooden spoon.

Drizzle the anchovy sauce over the warm beans, scatter over the parsley and chopped chilli pepper and serve.

SERVES 4 AS A SIDE DISH

Cozze ripiene
Stuffed mussels

While traveling along the trabocchi coast, we were invited to lunch at Ristorante Caldora, which sits on the water's edge near a few trabocchi at Punta Vallevò. Chef Marco Caldora invited me into his kitchen to see what he was cooking for our lunch. A wide and much-used frying pan sat on the gas stove, filled with a saucy red broth that was bubbling away. He was stuffing mussels with a mix of soft bread, semi-matured cow's milk cheese, egg, garlic and parsley and then dropping them into the sauce. I thought cheese seemed an unusual bedfellow for mussels, but Marco told me this was the Abruzzese way, combining elements of the farm and the sea.

The process of stuffing the mussels takes a bit of time – buy larger ones if you can – but it is time well spent, resulting in a surprisingly substantial and frankly delicious starter.

300 g (10½ oz) fresh mussels, cleaned and debearded (see page 17)

Tomato salsa

1 tablespoon extra virgin olive oil

½ brown onion, finely diced

400 ml (13½ fl oz) tomato passata or 1 x 400 g (14 oz) tin chopped roma (plum) tomatoes

sea salt and freshly ground black pepper

Stuffing

3 tablespoons grated aged pecorino

3 tablespoons grated parmesan

120 g (4 oz) crustless white bread, roughly torn

1 egg

1 tablespoon flat-leaf parsley leaves

To make the tomato salsa, heat the olive oil in a large frying pan with a lid over low heat, add the onion and cook for 10 minutes or until translucent and just starting to colour. Add the passata or tomatoes, making sure you add some water to the jar or tin to collect all the contents and pour it into the pan. Simmer for 20 minutes, then season to taste with salt and pepper.

Add the mussels to the salsa. Increase the heat to medium–high, then cover and cook for about 2 minutes, lifting the lid to check for open shells. Remove shells as they start to open with tongs and set aside, then replace the lid. Check again in 30 seconds and remove any shells that have opened. Repeat until all shells have started to open; after 5 minutes any shells that are still closed should be discarded.

(You can also steam open the mussel shells in a separate frying pan over high following the same method as above. Save the juices left into the pan and tip some of them into the salsa.)

To make the stuffing, place the cheeses, bread, egg, parsley and a couple of teaspoons of water (or 'mussel juice' if you have any left over from steaming the mussels in their own pan) in a mini food processor and process until the mixture clumps together, adding a bit more water if it is too dry.

Spoon the bread mixture into the open mussels and close the shells as much as you can (they will probably remain partly open). Arrange the shells in the salsa. If the salsa is looking a bit thick, add a few splashes of water.

Cover the pan and cook over low heat for 20–30 minutes until the stuffing is cooked through. Serve directly from the pan in the centre of the table or spoon the salsa into individual dishes and place the mussels on top.

SERVES 4 AS A STARTER

Calamari ripieni alla Pescarese
Stuffed calamari

Whenever my father had a choice of what to have for dinner he would invariably choose seafood, and he passed on his love of seafood to everyone in the family. My mother did all the cooking but he was the one who did the weekly shopping. I loved it when he bought calamari; Mamma would cut them into rings, dust them with flour and serve them quickly fried with a side of crisp homemade potato chips. She rarely stuffed them – maybe because it took longer and my father usually wanted dinner on the table early.

The people of Pescara have a delicious way of preparing stuffed calamari, and I am happy to share the recipe here. I would choose this over the quick-fried rings any time.

You can use squid or calamari for this dish – they are very similar. If you don't want to clean the tubes yourself, your fishmonger will usually oblige. Just make sure you take the tentacles and legs as they are an essential part of the stuffing.

4 medium calamari
(about 1 kg/2 lb 3 oz total),
cleaned (see page 16), tentacles
reserved

80 g (2¾ oz) crustless bread,
broken into small pieces

1 clove garlic, crushed

25 g (1 oz/⅓ cup) grated
aged pecorino

finely grated zest of
1 small lemon

1 teaspoon salted capers, soaked
in water for 10 minutes,
drained

2 anchovy fillets, finely chopped

1 tablespoon finely chopped
flat-leaf parsley

½ teaspoon freshly ground
black pepper

1 egg, lightly beaten

splash of milk (optional)

2 tablespoons extra virgin
olive oil

125 ml (4 fl oz/½ cup) dry
white wine

sea salt

Wash the calamari in a bowl of cold water, making sure the inside of each tube is clean and the entire quill has been removed. I like to trim about 5 mm (¼ in) off the pointy top of the tube so that no air is incorporated when you add the stuffing. This way you can also run water through the entire length of the tube, making sure the inside is well cleaned. You can trim the wings near the top of the tube, then cook them with the stuffed calamari, or keep them attached to the body. Set the washed tubes aside.

Divide each set of tentacles in half, setting aside half to cook with the stuffed calamari. Finely chop the remaining tentacles and place in a bowl to make the stuffing. Add the bread, garlic, cheese, lemon zest, capers, anchovies, parsley, pepper and egg. If the mixture is a bit dry, add a splash of milk.

Spoon the mixture into the tubes, taking care not to overfill them. Secure the wide end of each tube with a toothpick and pin the reserved tentacles to the tubes.

Pour the olive oil into a frying pan large enough to fit all the seafood and heat over medium heat. Add the stuffed calamari and cook for a few minutes until they change colour; the tentacles should curl immediately. Turn the calamari over and cook for a few more minutes until coloured, then add the white wine and allow it to cook off briefly. Reduce the heat and cook, covered, for 40 minutes or until the calamari is tender, turning occasionally so they cook evenly. Scatter on some salt to taste. If there is a lot of liquid in the pan, remove the cooked calamari and turn up the heat until it reduces. Strain the liquid through a fine sieve.

Cut each calamari tube into four or five slices and serve with the tentacles on the side. Finish with a drizzle of the strained pan juices.

SERVES 4 AS A STARTER

Zuppa ceci e castagne
Chestnut and chickpea soup

The smell of roasting chestnuts is one that many people associate with Italy. In colder months you will find giant pans of them roasting in piazzas and along the streets, filling the wintery air with an enticing aroma – a reminder that Christmas is around the corner. They are sold in a yellow paper cone and have a scorched skin and a sweet buttery texture. When chestnuts are not in season, Italians have made sure they are still available for cooking, in dried form, tinned or as a flour.

The Abruzzesi pair them with chickpeas in a thick and rustic soup, a great example of 'cucina povera' (poor man's cooking). I use fresh chestnuts and soaked dried chickpeas for this recipe, but if you want to speed up the process you can replace the dried chickpeas with about 600 g (1 lb 5 oz) of the tinned version. Similarly, you can use tinned chestnuts; if you do this, rinse them well and add them to the pan with all the ingredients.

You will need to start this recipe one day ahead

200 g (7 oz/1 cup) dried chickpeas

200 g (7 oz) fresh chestnuts

2 tablespoons extra virgin olive oil, plus extra to serve

1 clove garlic, finely chopped

1 brown onion, finely chopped

250 ml (8½ fl oz/1 cup) tomato passata

1 bay leaf

1 rosemary sprig

good pinch of chilli flakes

sea salt and freshly ground black pepper

crusty bread, to serve

Soak the chickpeas in plenty of cold water overnight. The following day, drain and rinse them well. Place them in a large saucepan, cover with water and bring to the boil. Simmer for about an hour until they are tender. Drain and set aside.

While the chickpeas are cooking, start preparing the chestnuts. Bring a saucepan of water to the boil, drop in the chestnuts and boil for 25–35 minutes until they are cooked through. The exact cooking time depends on the size of the chestnuts and you should start testing them after 25 minutes. To do this, scoop a chestnut out of the boiling water with a slotted spoon, let it cool for a minute or two and then peel it with a sharp knife. Chestnuts are difficult to peel once they cool so work quickly. Chop it in half and peel off both layers of skin. If it crumbles a bit, it's ready. When you are satisfied that they are cooked through, drain and peel the lot.

Select a saucepan large enough to fit all your ingredients, pour in the olive oil and heat over low heat. Add the garlic and cook until fragrant, then add the onion and cook for 10 minutes or until soft and translucent. Add the passata, bay leaf, rosemary, chilli flakes, drained chickpeas and peeled chestnuts. Add 500 ml (17 fl oz/2 cups) of water and bring to the boil, then reduce the heat and simmer for 30 minutes. Season to taste with salt and pepper.

Spoon into bowls and drizzle with really good extra virgin olive oil. Serve with crusty bread on the side. If you reheat the soup the next day, you may need to add a bit more water as it will thicken quite a bit once cooled.

SERVES 4

Maccheroni alla chitarra al Montepulciano
Spaghetti Montepulciano

L'Antico Feudo di Bracciale is an agriturismo just outside the town of Ortona, a few kilometres from the sea. It is run by the Bracciale family and includes a restaurant, accommodation and the farm. The farm is run organically and they produce most things they need to run the restaurant (olive oil, chickens, eggs, wine, vegetables, fruit); what they don't make or grow themselves they buy from nearby organic producers.

I first visited L'Antico Feudo in 2015 with my friend Giulia, who took me there to meet Fausto. Fausto's mother made us a spectacular pasta dish; the spaghetti was laced with Montepulciano d'Abruzzo wine and the meat sauce was tomato-free and very tasty. I remember us all mopping up the sauce in the central platter with chunks of bread.

When I was researching this book, Fausto invited me back for a 'laboratorio di cucina' (cooking lab) – his mother would make the famous Montepulciano pasta while I watched and took notes. When I told Giulia and her mother-in-law Francesca that I was going to get the recipe they both said, 'Ohhh we have been wanting to learn to make that for ages but she would never tell us how.' So here it is, including the recipe for the delicious sauce, for which I managed to get a list of ingredients and basic proportions. I worked out my own methodology; we Italian women are meant to have learnt our way around the kitchen from our mothers, and so cooking instructions are not needed when relaying a recipe.

chopped flat-leaf parsley and
finely grated parmesan, to serve

Pasta

300 g (10½ oz) superfine
semolina (semola rimacinata),
plus extra for dusting

2 eggs

3 tablespoons Montepulciano
d'Abruzzo wine (or your
favourite red wine)

Sauce

3 tablespoons extra virgin
olive oil

1 small white onion, finely diced

2 celery stalks and leaves,
finely diced

2 carrots, peeled and finely diced

400 g (14 oz) pure pork
sausages, casings removed,
meat broken into small pieces

sea salt and freshly ground
black pepper

To make the pasta dough, follow the instructions on pages 22–23 for making egg pasta, drizzling in the wine as you combine the flour and eggs and adjusting with water and/or flour if needed to obtain the right consistency. Cover and allow to rest for at least 30 minutes.

To make the sauce, heat the olive oil in a medium saucepan over low heat, add the onion, celery and carrot and cook, stirring occasionally, for 20–25 minutes until the vegetables are starting to soften. Add the sausage meat and stir well, then increase the heat to medium–low and cook for about 20 minutes until the sausage pieces are cooked through and have released their liquid. Add salt and pepper to taste.

While the sauce is cooking, make the pasta. Cut the dough into thirds. Working with one portion at a time, roll it out on a surface that has been lightly dusted with superfine semolina. You can use a pasta machine or rolling pin to roll it to a 3 mm (⅛ in) thickness. Place the rectangle of dough on the narrower strings of the chitarra and, using a rolling pin, press on the dough so that the metal strings cut it into strips. Dust the prepared pasta with superfine semolina and cover with a clean tea towel to prevent it from drying out. Repeat with the remaining dough. If you don't have a chitarra, dust the pasta with superfine semolina, then loosely roll it up and cut it into 3 mm (⅛ in) wide strips with a knife.

Bring a large saucepan of salted water to the boil. Drop in the pasta and cook until al dente (the cooking time will vary, depending on the thickness of the pasta). Drain, reserving a little of the pasta water in a cup. Toss the pasta through the sauce, either in the saucepan you cooked the pasta in or in a bowl, adding some of the reserved cooking water if it looks a bit dry.

Pile onto a serving platter, scatter with parsley and plenty of grated parmesan and serve.

SERVES 4

Sarde e patate
Sardine and potato bake

Sardines are so plentiful along the Adriatic coast that they can be cooked a dozen ways or more. They are a type of poor man's food – cheap, tasty and available all year round. This is an easy summer dish, with alternating layers of ripe tomatoes and thinly sliced potatoes, making it an attractive light meal or starter. It hardly requires any effort if you manage to buy the sardines already filleted; you'll have the dish on the table in well under an hour.

2 tablespoons olive oil

1 kg (2 lb 3 oz) fresh sardines, filleted (about 600 g/1 lb 5 oz fillets)

250 g (9 oz) potatoes, peeled and cut into 1–2 mm (1/16 in) thick slices

2 ripe tomatoes, seeds removed and roughly chopped

2 tablespoons dried breadcrumbs

1 teaspoon chilli flakes

2 teaspoons salted capers, soaked in water for 10 minutes, drained

2 tablespoons flat-leaf parsley leaves

sea salt

1 lemon, quartered

Preheat the oven to 180°C (350°F).

Drizzle 1 tablespoon of olive oil over the base of a medium baking dish. Cover with alternating sardine fillets and potato slices until they are finished. Scatter on the tomato, breadcrumbs, chilli flakes, capers and half the parsley, and season to taste with salt. Lastly, drizzle on the remaining olive oil.

Cover with foil and bake for 20 minutes, then remove the foil and bake for another 5 minutes. Scatter with the remaining parsley, squeeze over the lemon juice and serve warm.

SERVES 4 AS A STARTER OR LIGHT MEAL

Bietole, patate e seppie
Silverbeet, cuttlefish and potato bake

My friend Giulia runs a country house with accommodation, restaurant and a cooking school in Manoppello, about 25 kilometres (15 miles) from Pescara. She generously opens her doors to me when I am in Abruzzo, and makes me feel like I am one of the family. I stayed with her when I was researching this book, and kept picking her brain for traditional local recipes. One morning she surprised me with a gift: she had found a tiny booklet called Ci vo'. La Cucina Marinara Pescarese, which roughly translates to 'What You Need (as in, what ingredients you need) – Seafood Cooking from Pescara'.

The recipes are written in Abruzzese dialect, with the briefest of descriptions on how to make the dish – there are no quantities, and many are without cooking method and cooking times. So the recipe below is my interpretation of a dish in the book, one that I imagine the wives of fishermen would make to feed their hungry husbands after a night on the boat.

8 large silverbeet (Swiss chard) stalks

2 tablespoons extra virgin olive oil

½ brown onion, thinly sliced

2 potatoes, peeled and cut into bite-sized chunks

2 cuttlefish (about 500 g 1 lb 2 oz), cleaned (see page 16), cut into bite-sized pieces

sea salt and freshly ground black pepper

chilli flakes, to taste (optional)

Preheat the oven to 170°C (340°F).

Place a large saucepan of water over high heat and bring to the boil. Remove the thick white silverbeet stalks, then wash the leaves well and tear them into pieces. Plunge the leaves into the boiling water. When the water returns to the boil, remove the leaves with tongs and set aside in a colander to drain.

Now it's time to layer the ingredients in a round baking dish (mine was a deep terracotta dish with a 20 cm/8 in diameter). Drizzle 1 tablespoon of olive oil over the base, then add half the onion, half the potato and half the cuttlefish. Season with salt and pepper and sprinkle over a few chilli flakes (if using), then top with half the silverbeet leaves. Repeat with the remaining onion, potato and cuttlefish, drizzle on the remaining olive oil, and arrange the rest of the silverbeet leaves on top. They should cover the other ingredients completely. Season lightly with salt and pepper and cover with foil.

Bake for 1 hour, then remove the foil and bake for another 10 minutes or until the potato is tender. Allow to cool for a few minutes before serving.

SERVES 2 AS A MAIN OR 4 AS A LIGHT MEAL

Coniglio al tegame
Pan-cooked rabbit with capsicum

I went to lunch on a trabocco with my friend Emiliana, a generous and ardent advocate for her region of Abruzzo. When I was telling her about my book, and the mix of recipes I hoped to include, she suggested that having one or two rabbit dishes would reflect what the locals eat. My original plans to have a stuffed rabbit ('in porchetta') were thwarted when I could not find a butcher in my hometown of Melbourne willing to debone the rabbit (they actually laughed at me when I asked), and I was not game enough to try it myself. So I cut it back to one flavoursome dish: rabbit pieces cooked in a broth of garlic, herbs and lemon peel until the meat was falling off the bone.

Because rabbit has a fairly gamey taste (especially if wild-caught) I usually soak the meat in water and vinegar for a couple of hours before cooking. The roasted capsicum (bell pepper) draped on at the end replaces the dried sweet chilli pepper that is so common in dishes along the Abruzzese coast (I simply cannot find it in Australia). The soft red strips not only make a visual contrast but add a rich sweetness. This dish goes particularly well with a side of potatoes cooked any way you like, although my preference is garlicky roast baby potatoes with rosemary.

1 rabbit (about 1 kg/2 lb 3 oz), cleaned

150 ml (5 fl oz) white wine vinegar

sea salt and freshly ground black pepper

1 small red capsicum (pepper)

80 ml (2½ fl oz/⅓ cup) extra virgin olive oil

plain (all-purpose) flour, for dusting

2 cloves garlic, 1 crushed, 1 peeled and left whole

3 small rosemary sprigs, leaves picked, plus extra to garnish

4 sage leaves

2 small fresh bay leaves

2 cloves

2 strips lemon peel

125 ml (4 fl oz/½ cup) dry white wine

250 ml (8½/1 cup) warm water

your favourite roast potatoes, to serve

Using kitchen scissors or a knife, cut the rabbit lengthways through the centre, then cut it into 10–12 even-sized pieces, starting with the forelegs (which make a good-sized piece on their own). Take care with the bones as they can be quite small. Alternatively, ask your butcher to cut it into pieces for you. Place the rabbit in a large bowl and pour in the vinegar and enough water to cover. Allow to rest for 2 hours. Drain, rinse well, then pat dry and sprinkle lightly with sea salt.

Preheat the oven to 220°C (430°F) and line a baking tray with baking paper.

Cut the capsicum in half lengthways and remove the stem and seeds. Place on the prepared tray and roast for 20–30 minutes until the skin is slightly charred and the flesh is soft. Place in a plastic bag for a minute or so to allow the capsicum to sweat, then peel off the charred skin. Don't wash it or you will lose the lovely smoky flavour. Cut the flesh into strips about 5 mm (¼ in) wide.

Heat the olive oil in a large frying pan over medium heat. Dust the rabbit pieces with flour, then add them to the pan and cook for 5 minutes or until brown all over. Remove the pieces and set aside.

Add the garlic, herbs, cloves and lemon peel to the pan and cook for a few minutes until fragrant. Return the rabbit to the pan and increase the heat to medium–high. Add the wine and cook for several minutes, allowing most of the liquid to evaporate. Add the warm water and bring to a simmer, then reduce the heat to low and cover with a lid.

Cook for 45–55 minutes, turning the meat occasionally and making sure it remains moist and bathed in the cooking juices. Add a little more water if it starts to look a bit dry. Taste the sauce when the dish is almost ready and add salt and pepper to taste. The meat should be tender and falling off the bone.

Serve on a platter with roast potatoes, decorated with strips of roast capsicum and garnished with extra rosemary leaves.

SERVES 4

Fave fresche con uova e formaggio
Fresh broad beans with eggs and cheese

I was exploring my friend Giulia's vegetable garden, camera in hand, when I found her father-in-law Venturino crouched among the rows of broad (fava) beans. He was picking ripe pods and throwing them into a large pink wash tub. I offered to help and crouched down beside him, picking handfuls of long fleshy green pods. 'Adesso ne abbiamo abbastanza,' he said ('We have enough,') and carried the large tub into the kitchen, leaving me to my photography.

That evening at dinner time I was greeted by piles of broad bean pods, spilling onto the tablecloth. We each peeled our own, pairing the fresh beans with salty semi-matured local pecorino, and washed them down with Venturino's homemade red wine.

You can also cook fresh young broad beans, as I do here, combining them with leafy greens and eggs to make a superb weeknight dinner. It is an omelette of sorts, one that tastes of spring and reminds me fondly of Venturino.

2 tablespoons extra virgin olive oil, plus extra to serve

1 kg (2 lb 3 oz) young broad (fava) beans, podded (about 350 g/12 oz beans)

80 g (2¾ oz) young leaf chicory or spinach, washed and roughly chopped

2 spring onions (scallions), white part only, sliced

sea salt and freshly ground black pepper

6 eggs

100 g (3½ oz) pecorino, grated

25 g (1 oz) parmesan, grated

a mix of green leaves, to serve

Preheat the oven to 210°C (410°F).

Heat the olive oil in a large ovenproof frying pan over medium heat. Add the broad beans, chicory and spring onion and cook, stirring occasionally, for about 10 minutes until the beans are cooked through, adding a bit of water if needed. Season to taste with salt and pepper.

Place the eggs and cheeses in a bowl and lightly beat together. Add the egg mixture to the pan, making sure it spreads out evenly, and cook for 5 minutes or until the egg is cooked through. Briefly place the pan in the oven to set the top layer of egg.

Scatter the leaves over the top, drizzle with extra olive oil and serve straight from the pan, cutting it into wedges.

SERVES 4 AS A LIGHT MEAL

TRABOCCHI
ABRUZZESE FISHING MACHINES

The best time to see the row of trabocchi from Vasto looking northwards is at dawn.

Structures that you can just make out in the early morning light line the coast resembling spindly armed lobsters with claws and antennae facing seawards, reaching up to the sky. Local poet Gabriele d'Annunzio described the trabocchi 'fishing machine' as a colossal spider, having 'a life of its own, the appearance of a living creature'. In fact, they are quite fragile wooden piers with platforms and arms for fishing, built on promontories along the coast of Abruzzo. Wooden trabocchi are remarkably elastic and seem to move with the water.

TRABOCCHI
ABRUZZESE FISHING MACHINES

Many trabocchi are made from the wood of acacia trees, which grow tall and straight on the shores between Vasto and Ortona. Their gangly nature makes them vulnerable to damage by strong seas, winds and storms, and they frequently need to undergo repairs, like 'a person on whom age and suffering had taken its toll' (D'Annunzio).

A trabocco has a frail charm; it can never be more than temporary, and periodically needs rebuilding. In 1980 the trabocco Porta Tufano (yes, they have names, like boats) was completely lost, as its owner Rinaldo Verì explained to me as we sat on the trabocco he inherited from his father. Rinaldo believes that the first trabocco was built at Porta Tufano in the late 1700s, though he cannot be certain as no records exist; furthermore, he does not know how many times it has been destroyed and rebuilt. The oldest records he has indicate that one was dismantled in 1949 (and apparently transported to Tuscany by its then owner) and another was built on the same spot in 1962, of which he has a photo.

Rinaldo showed me a photo of his father Ettore and his father's friend Cesare, which was taken in August 1960, right where we were sitting; there was no trabocco at that time, but both Ettore and Cesare are standing on the back of a 19-metre (20-yard) whale! The story goes something like this: Ettore and Cesare were fishing with nets on their boat 'Fortunello' off the Adriatic coast near Punta Penna, when they saw a dark shadow that was larger than usual under a school of fish. They thought it was some sort of sea monster and rowed as fast as they could towards the shore. The creature followed them and beached itself right next to where the Porta Tufano trabocco currently stands, and there it remained until its death a few days later. It caused quite a stir, and photos of those days and the crowds that came to see the whale on the Abruzzese shore are framed and hanging on the trabocco.

Rinaldo is very proud of this story and of the way he runs his trabocco, largely as an educational point of reference for school and tourists groups to learn about the fishing machines on this stretch of coastline. He has resisted the urge to turn his trabocco into a full-time restaurant, which is the fate of most of the twenty-eight trabocchi between Vasto and Ortona. The trabocchi are often small, so some that have been converted into restaurants have their kitchens on the shore, with waiters dashing between the two, balancing plates of pasta and seafood along the trembling gangway that joins them.

While I was travelling, I heard the 'trabocchieri' (trabocco operators or fishermen) described as 'contadini di mare', or farmers of the sea. It is believed that it was not fishermen who originally built these fishing machines, but farmers who wished to supplement the meagre produce of their land with seafood, using these constructions to extend the land into the water. Rinaldo showed us the simple fishing technique of the trabocco: the antennae-like arms that reach skyward have fine mesh nets attached; a hand-cranked pulley system lowers the arms, and the nets fall into the water. It can take several men to operate the pulley system, more for hauling them out of the water than dropping them in. The trabocco may be 10–20 metres (yards) from the shore, so the waters where the nets are dropped are sometimes deep. A catch is reliant on favourable currents and the keen eye of a trabocchiere to spot a school of fish passing over the net, who must quickly gather the number of people required to swiftly heave up the nets and hopefully several dozen fish as well.

Typical varieties of seafood caught in a trabocco include cuttlefish, squid, anchovies, sea bass and bream, although most fish are on the small side. Fishing is quite rare as many trabocchi no longer have operational fishing machines, and since the advent of more commercialised fishing in the Adriatic Sea, the catches have reduced substantially. Sadly, water pollution close to the coast has also taken its toll.

What I found surprising, while talking to Rinaldo, was the realisation that each of the existing trabocchi is built on public land, meaning the trabocco owners may own the structure, but not the land on which it is built. Trabocchi require constant maintenance and by the 1990s, many had fallen into disrepair. Further south in Molise and the northern shores of the Gargano promontory, many of the few that existed have been abandoned or destroyed.

In recognition of the historic and cultural value of the iconic trabocchi, the Abruzzese government began financially supporting the existence of the trabocchi and granting licences to the owners of existing structures, thus ensuring their presence continues to attract tourists and serve as a reminder of local history. In the days of increased travel and dining out, the conversion of trabocchi to restaurants is a smart economic move and if truth be told, it is a unique and delightful experience to have a meal on a trabocco fishing pier. You might even like to think that the seafood you are eating in the spindly wooden restaurant was perhaps caught with the gangly arms and nets of the trabocco itself.

Foglie in padella
Pan-cooked greens

At the Agriturismo Antico Feudo in Ortona, I asked Matilde (the owner) which were the most popular traditional dishes they served at her restaurant. 'Our own chickens,' was the answer. 'Cooked alla brace (over an open fire), and grilled vegetables grown in our garden with pizza e foglie.' The 'pizza' is a type of poor man's bread, made with cornmeal or polenta, and the 'foglie' literally means 'leaves'.

The leaves are not just any leaves, but leafy greens, often bitter and usually found growing wild. Blanch them, then braise them quickly with garlic, chilli, anchovies and a good pinch of salt, then top the lot with really good extra virgin olive oil and you have the simplest and tastiest of dishes.

There are no wild leafy greens growing around my Melbourne apartment, but my greengrocer usually has leaf chicory, young silverbeet, broccoli rabe or broccolini, and I use one or more of these. I serve this as a side to most main meals in winter and early spring.

1 large bunch leaf chicory

1 large bunch broccolini

2–3 tablespoons olive oil

2 cloves garlic, finely chopped

3 anchovy fillets,
roughly chopped

1–2 dried hot chillies, chopped

sea salt and freshly ground
black pepper

extra virgin olive oil,
for drizzling

Wash and trim the chicory and broccolini, cutting the long chicory stems into thirds and the broccolini in half. Bring a large saucepan of salted water to the boil. Drop in the broccolini and cook for 2–3 minutes, then add the chicory and cook for another few minutes. Drain.

Heat the olive oil in a large frying pan over medium–low heat, add the garlic, anchovies and chilli and cook until they start to sizzle. Add the drained broccolini and chicory and warm through for about 5 minutes, tossing well. Add salt and pepper to taste, then drizzle with extra virgin olive oil and serve warm.

SERVES 6–8 AS A SIDE

Bocconotti
Chocolate pastry bites

Bocconotti come from the word 'boccone', which means 'a bite', so it's no surprise that these cakes are bite-sized. They were first made in Castelfrentano in the mid-to-late 1800s, to coincide with the first availability of dark chocolate. This was an expensive item so only the richer noble families could afford it, and of course it wasn't the ladies of the house who were making the bocconotti – it was their cooks. Bakers would bake their bread very early in the morning and, while the ovens were still warm, the cooks would bring their bocconotti to one of the two communal ovens in the town and produce these delightful chocolate pastry bites, with hints of almond and cinnamon. Several of the cooks making the bocconotti in Castelfrentano were related; so they shared the recipe among themselves and they are the ones who have passed the recipe down through the generations.

You will need to start this recipe one day ahead

125 g (4½ oz) dark chocolate (45% cocoa solids)

110 g (3¾ oz/½ cup) caster (superfine) sugar

3 egg yolks

120 g (4 oz) natural almonds, toasted and finely chopped

pinch of ground cinnamon

finely grated zest of 1 small orange

icing (confectioners') sugar, for dusting

Pastry

9 egg yolks

220 g (7¾ oz/1 cup) caster (superfine) sugar

180 ml (6 fl oz/¾ cup) extra virgin olive oil

70 ml (2¼ fl oz) Strega (an Italian liqueur) or sambuca

480 g (1 lb 1 oz) plain (all-purpose) flour, plus extra for dusting

Heat 300 ml (10½ fl oz) water in a saucepan until it is lukewarm. Add the chocolate and sugar and bring to the boil. Stir until melted and well combined, then remove from the heat and set aside to cool. Add the egg yolks and bring to just below boiling point, stirring constantly. Add the almonds and continue to stir, again bringing the mixture to just below the boil until it thickens (like a custard). Remove from the heat, stir in the cinnamon and orange zest and allow to cool. Cover and set aside cool completely overnight.

Preheat the oven to 170°C (340°F). Grease the base and sides of 12 x 120 ml (4 fl oz) muffin holes (or similar) with softened butter.

To make the pastry, place the egg yolks and sugar in a large bowl and beat with a whisk until well combined; add the olive oil, liqueur and flour and stir with a wooden spoon. The dough should be homogenous but quite soft.

With a spoon, take approximately 60 g (2 oz) of pastry and stretch it gently with your hands on a lightly floured work surface until it is around 5 mm (¼ in) thick. This will form the base of your bocconotto, so stretch it to the required size (I used a 9 cm/3½ in round cookie cutter). Place it in a muffin hole so that it just reaches the top, then repeat to fill the remaining holes, making sure the pastry adheres to the side.

Using a spoon, fill the pastry cups with the chocolate filling, making sure it reaches the top of the pastry. With the remaining pastry, use batches of about 30 g (1 oz) make small circles (approximately 7 cm/2¾ in) to cover the chocolate filling. Make sure your edges are sealed by carefully pressing all around the mould.

Bake for 30–35 minutes until the top of each bocconotto is golden. Remove from the oven and cool for 5 minutes, then carefully take them out of the tin and place them upside-down to cool. Once they have cooled, turn them over and dust with icing sugar.

Bocconotti will keep for a few days in an airtight container.

MAKES 12

Pizza di ricotta
Ricotta crostata

Every week I buy a large slab of fresh ricotta. It comes in its own drain basket so that I can easily separate the whey it releases. It reminds me of my father, who liked nothing more than to spread creamy ricotta and jam on a piece of toast for breakfast.

I have accumulated almost a dozen cake recipes that use ricotta and this one, which I found in Ci vo'. La cucina marinara Pescarese, *is my current favourite. It is called 'pizza di ricotta' per la Santa Pasqua, a sweet ricotta pie made for Easter celebrations. The term 'pizza' in Abruzzo and all through Puglia is a sweet or savoury pie rather what we generally think of as pizza.*

If you decide to make this cake for Easter Sunday, be sure to make it first thing that morning because it tastes even better when the ricotta has cooled completely, allowing you to really savour the aniseed liqueur in the pastry and the orange zest in the filling.

500 g (1 lb 2 oz) fresh ricotta, drained

2 eggs

125 g (4½ oz) granulated sugar

75 g (2½ oz) dark chocolate (45% cocoa solids), grated or finely chopped

100 g (3½ oz) natural almonds, finely chopped (not ground)

½ teaspoon ground cinnamon

finely grated zest of 1 small orange

3 tablespoons white rum

icing (confectioners') sugar, for dusting

Pastry

250 g (9 oz/1⅔ cups) plain (all-purpose) flour

1 scant teaspoon baking powder

pinch of salt

125 g (4½ oz) granulated sugar

1 egg

3 tablespoons milk

3 tablespoons extra virgin olive oil

1½ tablespoons aniseed liqueur such as sambuca

Preheat the oven to 170°C (340°F) and line a 21 cm (8¼ in) tart tin with a removable base.

To make the pastry, place the flour, baking powder, salt and sugar in a large bowl and whisk to incorporate. Drop in the egg, milk, olive oil and liqueur and stir with a wooden spoon until the dough comes together. You could also use a food processor.

Dust your work surface with flour and knead the dough for a minute or two until it is smooth. Cut the dough into two portions – you need two-thirds of the dough for the base and side, and one-third for the lattice top. Roll out the larger portion of dough between two sheets of plastic film to a thickness of 3–4 mm (⅛ in), to form a circle large enough to line the base and side of the tin. Carefully lift the pastry into the prepared tin, using your fingers to gently flatten it onto the base and side, cutting off the excess with a sharp knife. Wrap the remaining portion of dough in plastic film and rest in the fridge while you make the filling.

Place the ricotta, eggs and sugar in a large bowl and mix with a wooden spoon until smooth. Add the chocolate, almonds, cinnamon, orange zest and finally the rum. Stir until well incorporated, then spoon the filling into the prepared pastry case.

Roll out the remaining dough to a thickness of 3–4 mm (⅛ in). Cut the dough into strips (mine were just under 1 cm/½ in wide), then arrange the strips in a lattice pattern over the filling, gently pinching the ends to attach them to the pastry rim.

Bake for 50–60 minutes until the lattice is cooked through and golden. Set aside to cool completely.

Dust with icing sugar and serve cold. The 'pizza' will keep in an airtight container in a cool spot for 1–2 days, although the pastry will soften over time.

SERVES 10–12

4

LA RIVIERA
DEL CONERO

As you drive northwards along the A14, past the terracotta tiles of Civitanova Marche, the mass of Mount Conero abruptly appears on the skyline. Like many others, I had bypassed the region of Le Marche before, driving straight through it on the way from Abruzzo to Umbria. It is one of the lesser-known parts of Italy that only other Italians seem to know about, but it is a place of great beauty and solitude. It is in Le Marche that the Appenine Mountains meet the coast, with limestone cliffs dipping into the Adriatic Sea. Its hilltop towns rival those of Tuscany, with chequered fields of vines, olives, cherries and figs, and a riviera of beaches and fishing ports where traditional fishermen still fish at night and sell their catch in the morning on the beach.

We stayed in the tiny seaport of Numana, one of the three townships on the Conero Riviera. The high part of the town is called 'Numana Alta' and looks down onto the port and beaches that make up 'Numana Bassa', where yellow and white striped beach umbrellas form lines on the wide sandy beaches. From Numana Alta we could see fishing boats arrive and depart the port, and fishermen on the pier repairing their nets.

The treasure of the Conero Riviera is tiny Portonovo. The road in is the road out, and its buildings lean into the Adriatic from the very edge of the coastline, often stumbling onto the beach itself. Once, its isolation drew not only ascetics and religious Orders but also pirates, creating a need for garrisons to protect one and repel the other. And yet, throughout this time, the high rim of rock that embraces Portonovo with arms that reach all the way down into the clear waters of the Adriatic, has again and again mocked human endeavour and ambition with landslides that pushed people, buildings and entire forests into the sea, leaving only silence.

And now Portonovo is best known as the place to find Slow Food Presidia wild mussels (moscioli), and has restaurants, hotels, camping grounds and holiday houses. But it's all about the beaches, which are the template for the beach stereotype of popular fiction, with cliffs that skirt the clearest of sky-blue water, white pebbled shores and pine trees leaning as if to look into the water, as thoroughly entranced as the rest of us. To reach them, you have a take a boat. So sweet-talking a sea-faring local might get you to a hidden beach that everyone else can only peer at from the top of the cliff.

The food is richer than the more southern part of the Adriatic coast: eggs and meat are prominent in the cuisine here. At Campofilone, just south of the Conero Riviera, you will find a thin angel-hair pasta called macceroncini di Campofilone, made with soft wheat flour and eggs and generally eaten with a meat ragù. When I asked my host Monica, who lives in Numana, what typical dishes she and her husband eat, she reeled off an impressive and delicious list: tagliatelle pasta made with eggs, including stuffed ravioli; ragù made with duck or beef; a yeasty savoury cheese 'pizza' traditionally eaten at Easter; cured meats including prosciutto, lonza and coppa; stuffed rabbit for celebrations; and pan-cooked goat and chicken 'al potacchio'.

I found it interesting that although they live right on the water, they don't often eat seafood. This was echoed by Sandro, representative for the Slow Food Presidium for wild mussels and a native of Poggio. He explained that when he was little, although the town is not far from the coast, townsfolk seldom made it down that steep road to the water to fish, and fish-catches rarely made their way back up the road to the village. So his family ate the more traditional foods of the Marchigiani (people from Le Marche) much like Monica had described, but adding that they often ate preserved cod 'all'Anconetana' (in the style of Ancona).

I had been told that Porto Recanati, just south of Mount Conero, still had the feel of a fishing village, so I drove down the coast one morning and was just in time to see the last of the fishermen standing next to their boats, sorting through their catch on makeshift tables. Others were washing out their plastic buckets in the sea and cleaning their boats. There were a couple of tables on the walkway with ladies selling fresh seafood. Locals were cooing over a large basket of sea snails, saying they were going to cook them for lunch with ingredients like garlic, tomato, white wine and wild fennel.

I skipped the sea snails but I ate plenty of mussels: steamed in white wine, oven-baked with breadcrumbs and herbs, and combined with tomatoes over piles of spaghetti. Restaurants served up typical 'brodetto' (fish soup), containing many different types of seafood, cooked with saffron like they do at Porto Recanati to give it an unusual yellow colour and musky flavour.

The food we ate at restaurants was always accompanied by local wine, which has been a staple of Le Marche since Roman times. When Pliny the Elder wrote in the first century AD about the delicate aroma of the wines of Picenum, he was possibly writing about crisp green-toned verdicchio, or maybe about the full-bodied conero rosso, which grows on the lower slopes of Mount Conero. In addition to wine production, grapes are also used to make 'sapa' (also known as vincotto), a sticky sweet syrup with the slightest hint of acid. It is traditionally used in Le Marche and neighbouring Emilia-Romagna to add a sweet element to savoury dishes, such as a walnut pesto, or in a number of sweet dishes and cakes.

Salvia fritta in pastella
Fried sage leaves

Fragrant sage plants abound in the gardens of central Italy, and there is nothing nicer than having them fried in batter as an aperitivo. They are crisp and salty, and you always end up eating more than you planned to.

Look online and you will find many variations for the batter: whole eggs, egg whites or no eggs; beer, sparkling water or plain water; yeast or no yeast; rice flour, plain flour or even chickpea flour, or combinations of these. I have opted for the simplest version with plain flour and water, although rather than using tap water, I like to use sparkling. Once I accidentally picked up the wrong bottle and made these with lemonade; they had a delicious sweetness that I couldn't put my finger on until I went to drink from the bottle of 'water' and discovered my mistake. Since then I deliberately add a splash of lemonade to the batter. I also like to add a couple of ice cubes as I am frying the first few leaves, as the batter tends to thicken up over time. It also keeps it icy cold.

40–50 sage leaves

150 g (5½ oz/1 cup) plain (all-purpose) flour, plus extra if needed

1 tablespoon chilled lemonade

100 ml (3½ fl oz) iced sparkling water, plus extra if needed

olive oil, for pan-frying

sea salt flakes

Gently wash the sage leaves and pat them dry.

Place the flour in a deep bowl, add the lemonade and sparkling water and whisk to form a fairly runny batter that will still adhere to the leaves. Test by holding a leaf by the stem and dipping it in the batter, turning it from side to side. If necessary, adjust by adding more flour or sparkling water to achieve the right consistency.

Pour the olive oil into a small frying pan to a depth of 3–4 cm (1¼-1½ in) and heat over medium heat. It's ready when a small amount of batter dropped in the oil starts to sizzle.

Dip the leaves in the batter one by one and fry for about 20 seconds each side. I fry no more than two leaves at a time as you have to run them through the batter just before frying. They should puff up nicely and take on a golden colour. If they brown or burn or the oil starts smoking, reduce the heat.

Remove with a slotted spoon and drain on paper towel while you cook the rest.

Season with sea salt flakes and serve immediately.

SERVES 6 AS AN APPETISER

Moscioli gratinati con salsa di prezzemolo
Oven-baked mussels with flat-leaf parsley sauce

Mussels abound in the Adriatic. In seafood restaurants from Ancona to Civitanova you are likely to find everything from classic steamed mussels served with lots of pepper, to stuffed mussels and mussels in pasta sauce. If you are in the area between May and October you may find wild mussels that the locals call 'moscioli'. One of my favourite ways to eat them is 'gratinati', where these most tender of mussels are baked with a crunchy golden topping. This dish is particularly great in summer and I love to enjoy it with good friends and plenty of chilled verdicchio.

1.5 kg (3 lb 5 oz) fresh mussels, cleaned and debearded (see page 17)

125 ml (4 fl oz/½ cup) dry white wine

1 clove garlic, finely chopped

90 g (3 oz) dried breadcrumbs

2 plump tomatoes, seeds removed and finely diced

1 tablespoon finely chopped flat-leaf parsley

extra virgin olive oil, for drizzling

lemon wedges, to serve

Flat-leaf parsley sauce

20 g (¾ oz/⅔ cup) loosely packed flat-leaf parsley leaves

2 anchovy fillets

3 tablespoons extra virgin olive oil

1 teaspoon lemon juice

Preheat the oven to 200°C (400°F) and line two large baking trays with baking paper.

To make the flat-leaf parsley sauce, place the parsley, anchovies, olive oil and lemon juice in a small food processor and pulse until smooth, adding water if needed – it should be quite runny. Set aside. It may separate slightly on standing, so give it a good mix before serving.

Place a large frying pan with a lid over medium–high heat. Add the mussels and wine, then cover and cook for about 2 minutes, shaking the pan every 30 seconds or so. Remove the open shells and set aside. Replace the lid and cook the remaining mussels for another 30 seconds, then check again for open shells and remove those that have opened. Repeat a few more times, then discard any unopened shells after 5 minutes.

Strain the liquid left in the pan and reserve. Using a small sharp knife, separate the mussel meat from the open shells at the base of the stalk, trimming any beards that were missed in the cleaning process. Place the mussels in a bowl and set aside. Reserve 20–28 of the best half shells (or as many as you will be serving).

Place the garlic and breadcrumbs in a large bowl, then add enough of the reserved mussel liquid to bring the dry ingredients together. Stir in the tomato and parsley. You shouldn't need to add any salt as mussels are quite salty.

Heap a few mussels onto each shell half, then top with some of the gratin mixture. Drizzle with a bit of olive oil and place on the prepared trays. Bake for 10 minutes or until the crumbs are golden.

Serve warm with the flat-leaf parsley sauce and lemon wedges on the side.

SERVES 4 AS A STARTER

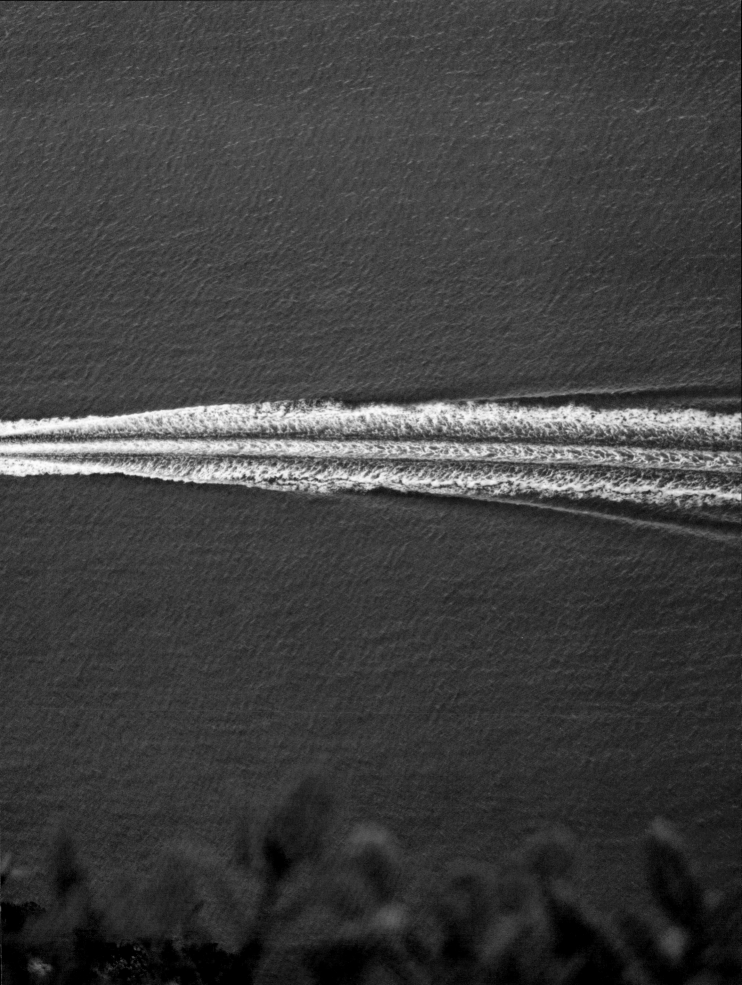

Pizza di formaggio Marchigiana
Easter cheese bread

During my travels through the Riviera del Conero, I stopped in Ancona and visited an osteria (tavern) that had been recommended to me. After a lovely seafood lunch I wandered the streets, taking photos, and chanced upon a bookstore. I went straight to the cooking section, looking for books about traditional cooking and found one that shared the stories and recipes of the women who once worked in the osterie of Ancona. In the opening pages author Carla Virili says she had been told that at the start of the 1900s there were a thousand osterie in the port town. Although she doubts the number is correct, the area had many small bars, taverns and kitchens that were as much about socialising as they were about eating and drinking wine. These were places that were nearly always frequented by men, port workers and fishermen, but often run by women, who cooked simple home-style meals. The recipes in the book generally don't have quantities, or much detail in the method, but are relayed in much the same way as they would when passing on a family recipe from mother to daughter.

This is a recipe for pizza di formaggio, a type of bread, usually eaten on Easter morning. It was inspired by Natalina, who once ran an osteria in Capodimonte, a section of Ancona.

4 teaspoons dried yeast

½ teaspoon caster (superfine) sugar

180 ml (6 fl oz/¾ cup) tepid milk

4 eggs

180 ml (6 fl oz/¾ cup) sunflower oil, plus extra for greasing

250 g (9 oz) bread flour

250 g (9 oz) plain (all-purpose) flour, plus extra for dusting

¼ teaspoon freshly grated nutmeg

½ teaspoon fine sea salt

100 g (3½ oz) aged pecorino, grated

100 g (3½ oz) parmesan, grated

70 g (2½ oz) fresh pecorino, asiago or Havarti cheese, cut into 5–6 mm (¼ in) cubes (optional)

Combine the yeast, sugar and milk in a small jug and set aside for about 10 minutes, until foamy.

Pour the yeast mixture into the bowl of an electric mixer fitted with a paddle attachment. Mix on low speed, then add the eggs one at a time followed by the oil, both flours, the nutmeg and the salt. When the mixture comes together, replace the paddle with a dough hook and knead on the second lowest setting for 2–3 minutes, until you have a sticky ball of dough. Tip in the grated cheeses and knead until the dough comes together.

Tip the dough onto a floured work surface. If using, toss the cheese cubes in a little extra flour, then knead through the dough with your hands. Keep kneading until you have a cohesive ball of dough, then place in a large oiled bowl, cover with a clean tea towel or plastic wrap and set aside in a warm draught-free spot for 2 hours or until doubled in size.

Line the base and side of a deep round 23 cm (9 in) cake or bread tin with baking paper.

Tip the risen dough onto your work surface and reshape by flattening it out with the palm of your hand, then folding the corners onto themselves. Place the dough, seam side down, in the prepared tin. Cover with a clean tea towel or plastic wrap and set aside in a warm draught-free spot again for 2 hours or until doubled in size.

Preheat the oven to 200°C (400°F).

Bake for 40 minutes or until golden on top and a skewer inserted in the middle comes out clean. Allow to cool slightly before removing the bread from the tin.

SERVES 10

Zuppa di ortiche
Stinging nettle soup

Foraging for foods, particularly wild greens, is very common all over the Italian peninsula. In spring, nettles are abundant and particularly tasty, and are a traditional herbal remedy for many ailments. They are also called 'vendetta delle suocere' (mother-in-law's revenge), referring to what might happen if lovers were to lie down in a field full of nettles …

While it may sound unlikely, this vibrant green soup is really lovely, rich in both colour and flavour. If you have trouble finding stinging nettles, it helps to ask around. I put out a call on social media when I was writing this book and at least three friends living in the country offered to give me bags of them as they were growing wild on their properties and they didn't know what to do with them. My cousin Emma collected a big bunch of the fragrant green leaves from a field next to her winery in the Yarra Valley and tied them up with a big string bow. I wasn't home when she tried to deliver them so she left them hanging off my door handle with a card saying, 'I don't think these are nettles but thought I would drop them over for you to check.' They were indeed nettles and when I called her to thank her she said she wasn't surprised as her hands had itched for at least half an hour after picking them! So remember to use gloves when handling the fresh leaves; cooking removes the stinging effect so you can touch them freely.

Give this soup a try – I know you'll love it. You'll wish you had an Emma nearby to bring you a bunch of nettles too.

2 tablespoons extra virgin olive oil

1 brown onion, finely chopped

100 g (3½ oz) stinging nettles, well washed

1 litre (34 fl oz/4 cups) vegetable stock

400 g (14 oz) potatoes, peeled and chopped

½ teaspoon freshly grated nutmeg

sea salt and freshly ground black pepper

grated parmesan, to serve

crusty bread or croutons, to serve

Heat the olive oil in a large saucepan over low heat, add the onion and cook for about 10 minutes until soft and translucent. Drop the nettles into the pan and cook for a few minutes. Add the vegetable stock and potato and bring to the boil, then reduce the heat and simmer for 20 minutes or until the potato is tender.

Using a stick blender, whizz the soup until it is fairly homogenous, although I like to leave a few chunks of potato for texture. Reheat gently, and season to taste with nutmeg, salt and pepper.

Ladle into bowls, sprinkle with parmesan and serve with crusty bread or croutons.

SERVES 4

Pasta sapa e noci
Pasta with grape must syrup and walnuts

As you drive northwards along the Adriatic coast, rows of vines become part of the scenery from the northern reaches of Puglia, through Molise, Abruzzo and into Le Marche. At the time of grape harvesting, in late summer and early autumn, sapa (vincotto), a cooked grape syrup, is made by reducing filtered grape juice over many hours. Sapa can be used in desserts but it also pairs well in savoury dishes with walnuts, which are ready to be harvested at the same time as grapes.

The sauce is a type of pesto, and should have an even balance of sweetness and nuttiness with a hint of acid. It is best suited to a short pasta like maccheroni or rigatoni so the sauce clings to it. Make sure you add plenty of parmesan to balance the inherent sweetness of the vincotto.

400 g (14 oz) dried short pasta
(such as rigatoni)

200 g (7 oz/2 cups) walnuts

2 tablespoons dried breadcrumbs
(preferably homemade)

80 ml (2½ fl oz/⅓ cup) vincotto

1 teaspoon balsamic vinegar,
or to taste

2–3 tablespoons extra virgin
olive oil

freshly ground black pepper

grated parmesan, to serve

Bring a large saucepan of salted water to the boil and cook the pasta until al dente, following the instructions on the packet. Drain, reserving a little of the pasta water in a cup.

Meanwhile, finely grind the walnuts in a mini food processor. Add the breadcrumbs, vincotto, balsamic vinegar, olive oil and pepper to taste and pulse until well combined. Taste to make sure it is balanced, adding a bit more balsamic if needed.

Return the pasta to the pan it was cooked in, along with a splash of the pasta water, and add the walnut sauce. Cook, stirring, over medium heat until the pasta is well coated and the sauce is warmed through. Divide among warmed bowls or plates and finish with a generous handful of parmesan.

SERVES 4 AS A STARTER

Tagliatelle con porcini e vongole
Tagliatelle with porcini and clams

I know this seems like an odd pairing. In fact, I chuckled when I first saw a porcini and clam pasta dish on the menu in a trattoria in Sirolo, wondering how you could possibly combine these two very different ingredients. But true to the Italian phrase 'mare e monti' (sea and land) they came together in style, with the earthy porcini perfectly complementing the delicate salty clams.

Take care when preparing the clams – they will need to soak for a few hours, and don't let them cook for longer than 10 minutes or they'll become chewy. If you can't find fresh porcini mushrooms feel free to use dried ones, or a mixture of dried porcini and fresh Swiss brown mushrooms.

1 tablespoon olive oil, plus extra for drizzling

1 clove garlic, peeled

400 g (14 oz) clams in the shell, cleaned (see page 17)

125 ml (4 fl oz/½ cup) dry white wine

300 g (10½ oz) fresh porcini mushrooms (or 50 g/1¾ oz dried porcini)

350 g (12½ oz) tagliatelle (if you want to make your own, see pages 22–23)

2 tablespoons chopped flat-leaf parsley

Heat the olive oil and garlic in a large frying pan with a lid over medium–high heat until the garlic becomes fragrant. Add the cleaned clams and the wine, and then cover and cook for about 1 minute, shaking the pan every 30 seconds or so. Remove the open shells and set aside. Replace the lid and cook the remaining clams for another 30 seconds, then check again for open shells and remove those that have opened. Repeat a few more times, then discard any unopened shells after 5 minutes.

Let the liquid left in the pan cool, then strain it through a fine sieve, removing the garlic clove and any sand. Return the liquid to the pan and set aside.

Remove the clams from the opened shells, discarding the empty shells. You could also keep the clams on the shells and serve them that way, though there's a good chance there will still be a little sand remaining.

If you are using fresh porcini, wipe them clean with a paper towel and remove the base of the stalk and any bruised sections. Cut the mushrooms into 3–4 mm (⅛ in) thick slices.

If you are using dried porcini, soak them in hot (not boiling) water for about 10 minutes. Discard the water as it will be too strong to add to the sauce. Cut the mushrooms into bite-sized pieces just before cooking.

Return the strained cooking liquid to low heat, add the fresh or dried porcini and simmer until tender. The fresh ones will need 10–15 minutes; the dried ones will only take about 5 minutes.

Bring a large saucepan of lightly salted water to the boil (remember that the clams will be quite salty so add less salt than you usually would). Cook the tagliatelle until nearly al dente – it will finish cooking in the sauce.

While the pasta is cooking, add the clams to the porcini mixture and warm through. Use tongs to drop the cooked pasta into the pan, stirring to coat well in the sauce and adding a little pasta cooking water if it looks dry. Cook for another minute or so, then divide among warmed bowls or plates, scatter with parsley and serve.

SERVES 4 AS A STARTER

Involtini di pesce in salsa
Fish involtini

From a personal, and perhaps selfish, point of view, I think there is room for more cabbage rolls in the world. We ate them often when I was growing up. My mother would arrange spoonfuls of rice, minced beef and herbs on firm cabbage leaves that had been blanched into submission, then deftly roll, fold and tuck them into neat little logs and place them in a pan. She called them 'involtini' and it was a clever way to get us to eat vegetables. We would eat them warm or even cold the next day if there were any left over.

These involtini were inspired by a lunch stop in an old osteria in Ancona, close to where I had miraculously parked the car (it was market day and there were road blocks and market stalls everywhere) but nowhere near my intended waterfront destination. Luckily the osteria had cabbage rolls on the menu. The filling had tender chunks of fish, crustless bread, garlic and a smattering of herbs, and the rolls were drenched in a rich tomato sauce. I recreated them at home, happily adding another cabbage roll recipe to my repertoire. They are reasonably child-friendly too – moist, tender and not too fishy.

8 medium cabbage leaves

1 tablespoon extra virgin olive oil

thyme sprigs, to serve

Salsa

1 tablespoon olive oil

1 clove garlic, cut into a few pieces

300 ml (10½ fl oz) tomato passata

sea salt and freshly ground black pepper

Filling

250 g (9 oz) red rock cod (or snapper or other firm-fleshed fish) fillets, skin and bones removed, cut into 6 mm (¼ in) cubes

100 g (3½ oz) crustless bread

1 small zucchini (courgette), coarsely grated

1 clove garlic, crushed

finely grated zest of 1 small lemon

2 teaspoons flat-leaf parsley leaves

½ teaspoon thyme leaves

½ teaspoon sea salt

1 large egg, lightly beaten

freshly ground black pepper

Preheat the oven to 180°C (350°F).

Bring a large saucepan of water to the boil and plunge in the cabbage leaves, a couple at a time (depending on the size of your pan) until they soften, then remove with tongs. When they are cool enough to handle, remove the thicker part of the central spine and dry the individual leaves with clean tea towels or paper towel. Set aside.

To make the salsa, pour the olive oil into a frying pan large enough to fit all the involtini. Place over medium–high heat and drop in the garlic pieces. Allow the garlic pieces to brown on all sides, then add the passata (take care as it may splatter). Reduce the heat to medium–low and cook for 10 minutes or until the garlic infuses the salsa. Remove from the heat, add salt and pepper to taste and set aside.

To make the filling, place the fish cubes in a medium bowl. Crumble or finely chop the bread and add to the bowl, along with the zucchini, garlic, lemon zest, parsley, thyme, salt and egg. Add pepper to taste and mix with a spoon (or your hands) until the mixture is well combined. Set aside.

Flatten a cabbage leaf on your work surface; you may need to trim a bit of the leaf to make it a squarish shape. Place a log of filling (about 50 g/1¾ oz) on one end of the leaf, then fold in the sides and roll it up as you would a parcel. Repeat until you have eight involtini. If you have any filling left over, don't waste it. You can shape it into a couple of tasty meatballs and cook them in the pan with a splash of olive oil.

Pour the olive oil over the base of a baking dish that will fit all the involtini in a single layer, then add them to the dish. Bake for 20 minutes. By this time the fish in the centre will have cooked through even though the cabbage leaves won't have changed very much.

While the involtini are baking, reheat the salsa over low heat. Using tongs, lift the cooked involtini out of the baking dish and place them in the frying pan with the warm salsa. Gently turn them so they are covered, and allow the sauce to infuse the cabbage leaves for a few minutes.

Serve the involtini warm, topped with salsa and garnished with thyme sprigs.

SERVES 4 AS A STARTER

Pollo in potacchio
Braised chicken

Monica, my host in Numana, told me that her nonna used to make the best 'pollo in potacchio', with a charred and crispy skin. She told me it had to be cooked over high heat on the stovetop, and even if you think the heat is too high, just keep going.

To make a traditional pollo in potacchio, the chicken must be cooked with very little sauce – the wine, tomatoes and chicken juices make the charred skin very tasty, while the inside remains surprisingly tender. Don't be tempted to put the lid on the pan and reduce the heat during cooking; stand near the stove and watch the chicken pieces cook, turning them over occasionally and adding a bit of water if needed. And certainly don't be tempted to add any wine from the glass you are holding as you make this dish – that is for you to enjoy while you breathe in the lovely aroma of the garlicky chicken.

4 chicken marylands
(or 4 thighs and 4 drumsticks)

3 tablespoons extra virgin
olive oil

4–5 cloves garlic

2–3 rosemary sprigs

125 ml (4 fl oz/½ cup) dry
white wine

125 ml (4 fl oz/½ cup) tomato
passata or 125 g (4½ oz) tinned
chopped tomatoes

sea salt and freshly ground
black pepper

Wash the chicken and pat dry with paper towel. Trim off any excess fat.

Pour the olive oil into a frying pan large enough to fit all the chicken and place over medium–high heat. Lightly crush the garlic with the side of your knife and add to the pan. As soon as the garlic starts to sizzle, add the chicken and rosemary. Cook on one side for 4–5 minutes until the skin has browned, then turn over and cook for another 4–5 minutes to brown the other side. Add the wine and allow that to sizzle and reduce for a few minutes, then add the passata or tomato and season with salt and pepper. The chicken will start releasing its juices and there should be a bit of liquid in the pan.

Continue to cook the chicken pieces, turning them over every few minutes so they cook evenly. If the pan becomes too dry and the chicken is sticking to the base, add a tablespoon or two of water. Cook until the juices run clear when the chicken pieces are prodded with a fork or the internal temperature of the largest piece of chicken is 75°C (165°F) according to a meat thermometer. The actual cooking time depends on the size of the chicken pieces, but it should be about 30–40 minutes.

Arrange the charred chicken pieces on a serving platter and spoon over the juices. This is delicious with your favourite mashed or roast potatoes.

SERVES 4

Capretto alla Marchigiana
Pancetta-wrapped goat

Easter is a time of celebration, and if you are dining with a family from Le Marche that likes to eat traditionally, this usually means goat or lamb will be on the table.

In this dish, pieces of goat shoulder are wrapped in thin slices of pancetta and baked with a breadcrumb topping. Goat has quite a gamey flavour, but you can reduce this by soaking the meat in a mixture of wine and water for about 30 minutes before you cook it. If you don't like the idea of goat or simply can't find any, you can replace it with skinless chicken thigh fillets, which are not traditional but will taste just as delicious.

750 g (1 lb 10 oz) boneless goat shoulder

250 ml (8½ fl oz/1 cup) dry white wine

2 tablespoons extra virgin olive oil

12 thin slices flat pancetta or bacon

4 sage leaves, roughly chopped

2 bay leaves, roughly chopped

1 rosemary sprig, roughly chopped

sea salt and freshly ground black pepper

125 ml (4 fl oz/½ cup) beef stock (preferably homemade)

30 g (1 oz) day-old bread (or homemade coarse breadcrumbs)

1 clove garlic, crushed

1 teaspoon finely chopped flat-leaf parsley

Trim off all visible fat from the goat meat and cut it into 12 even pieces. Place the meat in a bowl and add half the wine and 125 ml (4 fl oz/½ cup) water. Leave the meat to soak for 30 minutes, then drain and pat off all the excess liquid with paper towel.

Preheat the oven to 170°C (340°F).

Drizzle the olive oil over the base of a baking dish that will fit the goat snugly in a single layer. Wrap each piece of meat in a slice of pancetta or bacon and place in the dish. Scatter on the chopped sage, bay leaf and rosemary, then add salt and pepper to taste. Bake for 10 minutes. Remove from the oven and add 3 tablespoons of stock and 3 tablespoons of wine to the dish, then return to the oven and increase the heat to 180°C (350°F). Bake for another 10 minutes.

Meanwhile, break the bread into coarse crumbs using a mortar and pestle, or whiz briefly in a food processor. Mix with the garlic and parsley and set aside.

Remove the goat from the oven and drizzle the remaining wine and stock over the parcels. Scatter on the breadcrumb mixture and return to the oven for a final 10 minutes.

There will probably be quite a lot of juices left in the dish, particularly if you have used finer breadcrumbs. If so, remove the parcels from the dish and cover with foil to keep warm. Pour the juices into a small saucepan and simmer until reduced and thickened. Spoon the sauce over the warm parcels and serve.

SERVES 4

MUSSELS
WILD MUSSELS OF PORTONOVO

The 'moscioli selvatici di Portonovo' (wild mussels of Portonovo) have gained quite a reputation around the world since they were recognised by Slow Food (or Slow Fish) in 2004. The word for mussels in Italian is 'cozza', but the variety found in the region of Le Marche off the shore of Portonovo is almost exclusively called 'mosciolo'. It is a symbol of the area and part of the local identity.

MUSSELS

WILD MUSSELS OF PORTONOVO

Mussels have been farmed in Europe for centuries; in fact, most of the mussels on the worldwide market are farmed. Mussel larvae attach to ropes floating in the water and once they have grown a couple of centimetres, they are collected and suspended in the sea in sleeves and left to grow until they are large enough to eat. 'Moscioli' (wild mussels), on the other hand, are fished from rocky shelves or reefs a few metres (yards) below the water level, off the coast just south of the port town of Ancona. Crystalline waters and the configuration of the rocky shelves mean that the tides form a vortex, allowing the newly produced mussel seed to easily attach in the same area, rather than being washed away.

Sandro Rocchetti is a local of nearby Poggio, and a representative of the Slow Food Presidium for wild-caught mussels at Portonovo. I met with him at the start of the mussel season, which runs from May to October. 'You might be in luck,' he said. 'I think the boat has just pulled in.' We walked through Portonovo Pesca (the local fish shop) and out onto the shore, just in time to see two men unloading bags of mussels from a small boat. The boat had left at daybreak with a driver and a diver, and returned some four hours later with a large haul of wild-caught mussels. The diver plays the role of the 'mosciaiolo' (mussel man!), and dives underwater to scrape the mussels off the reef with a small rake. He puts them in meshed sacks and swims up to the boat, where they are sifted. Sifting allows any immature mussels or mussel seeds inadvertently collected to drop back into the water and onto the reef to re-attach. This is very important, explained Sandro, as it means the reef is constantly being replenished, making it completely sustainable. This is what makes the mussels of Portonovo so unique and it ensures that, in spite of frequent but controlled fishing during the peak season, there are always plenty of mussels growing.

Massimo, the mosciaiolo, swims to the reef many times during each trip to collect the mussels. 'It is hard work,' he told me. 'And there are not many willing to do it, as the days are long, and there aren't many people to talk to out there.' Once collected, sifted and bagged, the mussels are kept cool on the boat before arriving back on shore. The moscioli are sold from the tiny Portonovo Pesca shop, or transported to nearby Numana for sale.

Massimo opened one of the just-caught shells with a small knife. 'See this one? The flesh is orange or pink, and this means it is a female. Male mussels have white flesh.' Mussels survive about five days after being fished and must be stored in the fridge and cooked while still alive.

To check whether the mussels you have are alive, look at the shell: it should be tightly shut. If it is open, tap on the shell and see if it shuts. Shells that remain open contain dead mussels and should be discarded.

The region is one of the largest natural mussel-growing areas in the world. The majority of mussels that we eat are grown in nets in the ocean, where, as Sandro explained, the quality can be inconsistent due to the shape of the net or sleeve in which the mussels grow. The moscioli are celebrated in the area with an annual 'sagra' (festival) called 'Mosciolando', which is held in June. The locals are very proud of their mussels and believe they are the best in the world. There is something so special about eating mussels that grow naturally in the wild and are completely sustainable. Their peak is in July and August, when they are plump, firm and at their absolute sweetest.

I was interested to hear that mussels have not always been part of the local cuisine in this part of the Adriatic. At the start of the last century, farmers from hillside towns on the Conero started searching for other means of feeding their families and took to the sea in oared boats, collecting mussels from the reefs off the shores of Portonovo. Sometimes they would eat them raw, straight from the sea.

Sandro had arranged for us to eat at Da Emilia, a family-run restaurant and one of the oldest in Portonovo. Federica manages the dining room and she talked about her grandmother, nonna Emilia, who originally opened the restaurant. Emilia was living in Poggio on the mountain above and in the late 1920s she started taking simple lunches to groups of people who were visiting the beach. Rather than bringing food down from Poggio she eventually built a small restaurant and in 1950 moved to the current site, adjacent to the Portonovo Pesca shop. One wall of the restaurant is covered with old black-and-white photos. They are images of Emilia and her family and friends, and they show her passion for food and for the beautiful beachside location of the restaurant with Mount Conero as its backdrop.

Sandro suggested we try three courses of mussels, which is exactly what we did: plump mussels marinara style, lightly steamed and simply dressed with olive oil and parsley; shredded mussels sitting atop a pyramid of spaghetti, with a touch of tomato and parsley; and 'gratinati' (au gratin), oven-baked with a golden topping of breadcrumbs. It was an absolute feast and as we ate we looked out at the bluest sea, watching the boat take off towards the reef for another collection of mussels.

Brodetto di pesce di osteria
Osteria fish stew

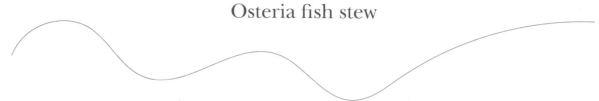

If there is one dish that you find along the entire coast of the Adriatic, it is 'brodetto' (which translates as the slightly less romantic 'fish stew'). Brodetto comes from the word 'brodo', meaning broth, as it always has lots of pan juices.

Brodetto varies from town to town, using different types of seafood and accompanying ingredients. This one is based loosely on one in Carla Virili's book Sapori d'Ancona (Flavours of Ancona), which shares the stories and recipes from the women who ran osterie in Ancona, serving home-cooked meals and wine for the locals.

This recipe is like Irma's, who ran an osteria in the middle of the port of Ancona, with tables for patrons in a vine-covered garden. She suggests adding the squid or cuttlefish at the same time as the onion base. This means that rather than remaining obstinately rubbery, the squid yields and becomes tender after the longer cooking time. At Irma's osteria, plates would arrive back in the kitchen almost clean, as the sauce on the plate had been completely mopped up by appreciative patrons. I think you will also want to mop your plate clean when you try this brodetto.

Use whatever seafood is fresh, and use several kinds. If in doubt, ask your fishmonger what he would recommend to make a brothy fish stew.

1 kg (2 lb 3 oz) your favourite seafood (squid, mussels, clams, prawns (shrimp), monkfish/stargazer, sea bass)

3 tablespoons virgin olive oil

1 brown onion, diced

1 clove garlic, finely chopped

1 teaspoon chilli flakes (or to taste)

3 tablespoons white wine vinegar

large pinch of saffron threads dissolved in 1 tablespoon water

1 x 400 g (14 oz) tin good-quality tomatoes

3 tablespoons flat-leaf parsley leaves

sea salt and freshly ground black pepper

crusty bread, to serve

See pages 16–17 for instructions on how to clean the various types of seafood; larger fish should be purchased already filleted, with skin removed. Remember that if you are including clams you'll need to allow 3 hours of soaking time. As a general rule, aim to have everything in bite-sized pieces, although I would recommend leaving prawns whole and still in their shell.

Heat the olive oil in a large frying pan with a lid over medium–low heat. Add the onion, garlic, chilli and any cephalods (squid, octopus, cuttlefish). Cook for about 10 minutes, stirring occasionally, until the onion is translucent. Increase the heat to medium–high and add the vinegar. Cook for a few minutes, then add the tomatoes, including the juice in the tin, breaking up any whole tomatoes with a wooden spoon. Bring to a simmer, then cover, reduce the heat to medium–low and cook for about 15 minutes.

Once the tomato sauce has thickened, add half the parsley and then start adding the fish, larger pieces first (monkfish/stargazer, sea bass), then the cleaned mussels or other large bivalves. Prawns and small bivalves such as clams should be added last. Cook for 10–15 minutes until the fish is cooked through, the bivalve shells have opened (discard any closed ones) and the crustaceans have changed colour. Taste the sauce and add salt and pepper if needed. The dish should be quite soupy but if there is too much liquid in the pan, increase the heat briefly and simmer uncovered to allow the excess to evaporate. Scatter on the remaining parsley before serving.

Serve directly from the pan with plenty of crusty bread to mop up the pan juices. You could also serve it with soft polenta (see page 14).

SERVES 6

Salame di fichi
Fig and nut roll

Figs grow abundantly in the Vallesina, just north of Ancona, and they are traditionally used to make a dried fig and nut roll known as a 'salame' or 'lonzino di fichi'. The term 'lonzino' literally means 'small loin', a slightly odd name but it probably refers to the shape of the roll. It is made in autumn, when fig trees are heavy with ripe fruit. The picked fruit is dried in the sun, mixed with finely chopped nuts then laced with aniseeds, cooked grape must and a bit of rum. It is shaped into a log, a bit like a salami, then wrapped in a large fresh fig leaf and tied with string to preserve it for use through the year. If you are fond of liquorice (like I am) you will find the aniseed overtones of the log quite irresistible; and if you want to go a step further (like I do) you can replace the rum with aniseed liqueur. I keep the roll in the fridge until ready to serve, and then cut into thin rounds to accompany a sharp cheese.

Fresh figs are seasonal and expensive so my version is made with good-quality dried figs, which you can find all year round. Try to find softer dried figs that yield slightly when you press on them.

300 g (10½ oz) dried figs
(a softer variety if possible)

30 g (1 oz) blanched almonds,
toasted, roughly chopped

30 g (1 oz) walnuts,
roughly chopped

30 g (1 oz) hazelnuts, toasted,
roughly chopped

1 tablespoon vincotto

1 tablespoon white rum
or aniseed liqueur

½ teaspoon aniseeds, crushed

If your figs are very hard and dry, soak them in hot water for about a minute to soften them slightly, then drain. There's no need to do this if they yield slightly when you press on them.

Roughly chop the figs and place them in a food processor with the remaining ingredients. Pulse until a thick paste forms, adding a little water if the mixture is dry.

Divide the mixture into four even portions. Place each portion on a small piece of plastic film and form into a 10 cm (4 in) log. Chill for several hours before cutting into rounds to serve. The wrapped logs can be stored in the fridge for a month or so.

MAKES 4 LOGS

Biscotti del pescatore
Fisherman's biscotti

Biscotti del pescatore are found in bakeries along the coast of Le Marche; mounds of nutty pastry studded with sultanas perfumed with a hint of rum. They are made without any fuss and keep well in a tin, forgotten for a few days only to be retrieved and dunked happily in a cup of milky morning coffee. Although they typically contain pine nuts, I like using hazelnuts instead (more to do with what is in the pantry than by design), but you can experiment with your favourite nuts. Just remember to toast them – it really does make a difference to the flavour – and keep the quantities the same. My friend Vanessa, who tested the recipe for me, told me she loved the biscotti so much that she ate five that day for breakfast, one after the other.

2 eggs

140 g (5 oz) caster (superfine) sugar

330 g (11¾ oz) plain (all-purpose) flour

2 scant teaspoons baking powder

pinch of salt

80 g (2¾ oz) butter, at room temperature

1 teaspoon vanilla essence

25 g (1 oz) hazelnuts, toasted, finely chopped

25 g (1 oz) natural almonds, toasted, finely chopped, plus extra whole almonds to decorate

25 g (1 oz) walnuts, finely chopped

40 g (1½ oz) sultanas (golden raisins) soaked in grappa for at least 30 minutes

Preheat the oven to 170°C (340°F) and line two large baking trays with baking paper.

Beat together the eggs and sugar in a bowl, then add the flour, baking powder, salt and butter and combine energetically using a whisk. (You could also do this with a food processor.) Add the vanilla, nuts and drained sultanas and stir until well combined. The mixture will be quite thick.

Form the dough into walnut-sized balls, then flatten them slightly and press a whole almond into the top of each one. Place them on the prepared trays, leaving plenty of room for spreading, and bake for 20–22 minutes until golden. Allow to cool for a few minutes, then transfer to a wire rack to cool to room temperature. The biscotti will keep in an airtight container for a couple of days.

MAKES ABOUT 35

5

LA DELTA DEL PO

The Po River weaves through wetlands and parklands on its way to the Adriatic Sea, dividing the region of Veneto from Emilia-Romagna to its south. The river branches into a series of canals and lagoons, criss-crossing parklands and marshes, and is home to hundreds of species of birds. On the drive along the coastal road, you will pass wide sandy beaches, brackish lagoons, low-lying salt pans, fishing huts, pine forests and towns with canals that remind you a little bit of Venice.

Bologna in central Emilia-Romagna is known as 'La Grassa' (the fat, or rich one) for its cured meats and heavier pasta dishes, but on the lesser-known eastern perimeter, the foods reflect the wildlife and produce of the low-lying valleys and waterways. In the town of Ravenna, famous for its Byzantine heritage, you will find 'cappelletti', a type of filled egg pasta that is often served in a rich clear broth; in inland Bologna the cappelletti are mostly filled with meat but in Ravenna and along the coast you will more often find them filled with ricotta and parmesan. And so it is with 'passatelli', a type of pasta made with breadcrumbs, eggs and parmesan that float in a broth. In the centre of the region it's a beef broth, but along the coast it's fish.

We stayed in Ravenna, a short drive from the coast, and every day I would drive towards the sea, stopping to visit a lady called Mirella. She runs a food truck parked by a canal, and I would always stop for a mid-morning 'piadina', a warm filled flatbread that is typical of the area. I would stroll along the canal as I ate, towards a small wooden 'capanno da pesca' (fishing hut). The hut has a small garden bursting with red poppies, and is perched on stilts a couple of metres (yards) above the waterway. Down the length of the canal, there is a row of capanni with spindly arms and nets reaching over the water. One day I saw one of the 'capannisti' (fishing hut owners); he was sitting on a platform at the water-facing end of his hut, with the net lowered into the water. Dozens of birds were looking on, poised for the net and its catch to be flipped into the air.

The wetlands of the Po Delta are dotted with 800 or so capanni, which were once made of reeds harvested from the canals, but are now made of wood. Although you can see them from the road, many can only be reached from narrow unpaved private roads, with boom gates to deter lookers-on. The richness of wildlife has always attracted hunters and fishermen, and the capanni served as a place to store fishing and hunting equipment, rather than being a fishing device (like the trabocchi of Abruzzo and Molise). Nowadays the capanni are more likely to serve as country weekenders for those from nearby towns: a day of fishing that ends with freshly grilled sardines or shrimp, well salted and drizzled with lemon, enjoyed with a glass of wine and a group of friends around a makeshift table.

The lagoon town on Comacchio is built on small inter-connected islands. Its pale pink and lemon houses, narrow canals and grand bridges echo the architecture of the islands in the Venetian Lagoon. Eels are the mainstay of the town and 'la sagra dell'anguilla' (the annual eel festival) is celebrated every July. When we visited I ate delicious chunks of grilled eel, and a traditional eel risotto drizzled with lemon.

The low-lying lands of the river delta are filled with wildlife and flora. Climb one of the wooden watch towers scattered through the parklands and you will see flocks of birds dipping and diving in the sky before landing on the water between the tall reeds. Hunting has long been a tradition around the delta, particularly in autumn and winter, and equipment would be stored in the casoni or capanni. Typical catch includes quail, pheasant and duck – usually roasted or cooked on the spit – as well as hares and rabbits.

The marshy patches of green are fertile with an abundance of wild flowers, herbs, fruit and vegetables. Violet 'prugnoli' (blackthorn) are used to make a spicy liqueur called prugnolino, and lanky tufts of wild asparagus are served with a sauce made with hard-boiled eggs and anchovies. Stinging nettles grow wild, along fields, ditches and gardens – their vibrant colour and flavour making them ideal for omelettes or risotto, as a filling for tortellini or for making fragrant green egg pasta.

Alici alla leccarda
Baked anchovy fillets with lemon

On our first night in Ravenna, our host Gabriella recommended we go to her favourite restaurant, Antica Trattoria al Gallo. She rang ahead and even though it was fully booked, they just managed to fit us onto their corner table. It was an old-fashioned place, with faded prints on the wall and an air of quiet refinement, making me wish I had worn a nice dress rather than utilitarian jeans. The owner took us on a quick tour of the many-roomed trattoria to show us the statues, chairs and other antique furniture he had bought at auctions over many years. The restaurant has been in the family since 1909 and the food is traditional, served on finely decorated plates by serious-looking wait staff. This recipe was inspired by one of the dishes I ate as an appetiser – delicate fresh anchovy fillets, barely warm and dotted with tiny cubes of carrot, strands of dill and crushed red peppercorns.

If preferred, you can replace the anchovies with the smallest sardine or mackerel fillets you can find.

32 small fresh anchovy, sardine or mackerel fillets

1 tablespoon mild extra virgin olive oil

juice of 1 lemon, plus extra if needed

2 teaspoons finely diced carrot

1 teaspoon red peppercorns, lightly crushed

2 teaspoons dill fronds

1 tablespoon chopped flat-leaf parsley

sea salt and freshly ground black pepper

Preheat the oven to 170°C (340°F).

Check the fish fillets and remove any remaining bones. Drizzle the olive oil over a baking tray that will fit all your fillets and place them skin-side down (it's fine if they overlap). Drizzle on the lemon juice, scatter over the carrot, peppercorns, dill fronds and half the parsley, and season lightly with salt and pepper.

Cover with foil and bake for 15–20 minutes, checking halfway through to make sure the fillets are covered with liquid; if not, add a bit more lemon. You will know they are cooked when their flesh is firm and looks opaque.

Serve warm, drizzled with some of the cooking liquid and finished with the remaining parsley.

SERVES 4 AS AN APPETISER

Passatelli in brodo di pesce
Passatelli in fish broth

While visiting the salt pans of Cervia, I tagged along with a school excursion group and sat next to one of the teachers, Raffaella Evangelista, on the short bus trip to the salt factory. I explained that I was writing a cookbook and she eagerly volunteered a family recipe. 'Passatelli,' she said, 'We eat them in a fish broth.' I listened with interest as she listed the ingredients, as I had tried passatelli in a chicken broth before but never with fish. To make passatelli you use a special contraption, which looks like the bowl of a giant slotted spoon with handles. You scrape the convex part onto a firm mound of dough made with breadcrumbs, egg and parmesan, causing noodles of the dough to be pushed up through the holes. If you don't have a passatelli maker (I don't either), you can use a potato ricer with larger holes for a similar effect.

Fish broth is quite easy and cheap to make if you know a good fishmonger. Fish shops often have a lot of spare fish heads and spines, as they are forever preparing the fillets and discarding the rest. Let them know you are making broth and you might get a few free of charge. If you don't like fish, you could enjoy the passatelli with chicken or vegetable broth instead.

1 large fish head and spine (or those from several smaller fish)

½ carrot, peeled and roughly chopped

½ white onion, roughly chopped

½ celery stalk, roughly chopped

2 flat-leaf parsley sprigs

1 ripe tomato, roughly chopped

sea salt and ground white pepper

Passatelli

130 g (4½ oz) dried breadcrumbs

130 g (4½ oz) parmesan, grated

2 large eggs

finely grated zest of 1 lemon

Wash the fish head and bones and place in a large saucepan. Add the carrot, onion, celery, parsley and tomato and cover with water – you'll need about 1.5 litres (52 fl oz). Bring to the boil, then reduce the heat, cover and simmer for about 45 minutes. Remove the fish pieces and vegetables with tongs, then pass the broth through a very fine sieve or piece of muslin. Pour the broth into a clean medium saucepan and cook for another 15–20 minutes until it has reduced sufficiently and the flavours have intensified – you will need to taste it to determine this. Add salt and white pepper to taste.

To make the passatelli, place the breadcrumbs, parmesan, eggs, lemon zest and 1 tablespoon of the fish broth in a bowl and mix well with a spoon or with your hands until it forms a rather stiff but pliable dough. Add a bit more of the broth if needed to bring the dough together. Wrap it in plastic film and let it rest for 15 minutes.

Push the dough through the passatelli maker or the widest plate on your potato ricer to make thick worms of dough, 2–3 cm (¾–1¼ in) long. Take care as they can be quite delicate. If they crumble, you may need to add a bit more broth to the dough. You can easily put the crumbs back into the passatelli maker or ricer if needed and remake them.

Bring as much broth as you think you will need to a steady simmer (you can freeze the rest). Carefully tip the passatelli into the broth and cook just until they float to the surface – this should be no more than a couple of minutes. Ladle into bowls and serve immediately.

SERVES 4

Cappelletti di Ravenna in brodo
Cappelletti in chicken broth

The words Italians use for their more unusual pasta shapes can be quite literal: 'radiatori' (radiators) come to mind, as do 'conchiglie' (shells) and 'acini di pepper' (peppercorns). In Emilia-Romagna they make 'little hats' (cappelletti), a circle or square of dough that is filled, then folded into a circular hat shape. The more opulent version from the central part of the region has them filled with meat, whereas in Ravenna they have them 'al magro', the lean version, filled with cheese instead.

The Bolgnesi like to eat cappelletti with a slow-cooked meaty ragù but I prefer them in an old-fashioned chicken broth, like we have at home for Easter Sunday lunch. The broth is special; it is made using a whole organic chicken, chopped into pieces and cooked for at least 3 hours. The broth is pale golden and sumptuous in its own way, a fitting soup for the 'al magro' cappelletti.

Cappelletti are rather a lot of work, but once you get into the groove of making them, make a big batch and freeze some for another time. This recipe makes about 60 cappelletti, which will serve four as a main, or eight as a light meal or starter. Start the broth the day before you want to serve. If you don't have time to make it from scratch, purchase good-quality broth from your local deli or chicken shop.

You will need to start this recipe one day ahead

superfine semolina
(semola rimacinata),
for dusting

Chicken broth

1 x 1.2–1.4 kg
(2 lb 10 oz–3 lb 2 oz)
organic chicken

½ carrot, peeled and
roughly chopped

1 celery stalk, roughly chopped

½ brown onion, peeled

Pasta

2 eggs

200 g (7 oz) 00 flour or
plain (all-purpose) flour

Filling

240 g (8½ oz) parmesan, grated

120 g (4 oz) fresh ricotta,
drained

good pinch of freshly
grated nutmeg

1 small egg, lightly beaten

freshly ground black pepper

To make the broth, chop the chicken into 8–10 pieces and remove as much of the skin as you can (this might be a bit difficult around the wings so it's fine to leave some). Wash the chicken and place in a pressure cooker, then add the vegetables and cover with water. I fill my pressure cooker to the 4-litre (140 fl oz) line, which is its maximum capacity. Cook the chicken on high for 1 hour, then set it to slow pressure release – it will take another 45–60 minutes to release its pressure.

If you don't have a pressure cooker, place the chicken and vegetables in a large saucepan or stockpot and add 2.5–3 litres (87–105 fl oz) of water. Bring to the boil, then skim off any impurities that come to the surface. Reduce the heat and simmer for at least 3 hours.

Remove the chicken and vegetables from the stock and allow it to cool to room temperature. Strain through some muslin or a fine sieve into a large bowl, then cover and place in the fridge overnight. The next day, you will see that a layer of fat has formed on top of the broth. Carefully scoop this out and discard. The broth is now ready to use or freeze for another day.

To make the pasta dough, follow the instructions on pages 22–23 for making egg pasta. Cover and allow to rest for at least 30 minutes.

To make the filling, place the cheeses and nutmeg in a bowl and mash them together with a fork. Add as much egg as you need to make a thick paste (discard any remaining egg or keep and use it for something else). Season with pepper (no need for salt) and set aside.

Dust your work surface with superfine semolina. Cut the pasta dough in half and wrap one half in plastic film while you roll out the other portion. Using a pasta machine, roll out half the dough until it is quite thin (I took mine to the second last setting of my machine).

Using a 6 cm (2½ in) or 7 cm (2¾ in) ravioli cutter, cut out circles of pasta. Place about ½ teaspoon of filling in the centre of each circle. Dip your finger in water and dampen the edge of the dough, then fold it over into a semi-circle, pressing down carefully so as to not incorporate any air. Next, fold the two corners of the semicircle onto each other, pressing to seal, then fold down the rounded part of the semicircle to make the hat-like brim of the cappelletto (see the photo on page 196). Cover the finished cappelletti with a clean tea towel and repeat with the remaining dough and filling. You should have about 60 cappelletti at the end. At this point, you can freeze the cappelletti in freezer bags if you like.

To serve, bring as much broth as you need to the boil and drop in the cappelletti. Once the broth returns to the boil, reduce the heat and simmer until the cappelletti are cooked through (the cooking time will depend on the size, but start checking at about 4 minutes). Ladle into bowls and serve hot.

SERVES 4 AS A MAIN OR 8 AS A STARTER

Gnocchi con erbe e formaggio di fossa
Gnocchi with mixed greens and cave-ripened cheese

In Solignano al Rubicone in Emilia-Romagna, just north of Le Marche, they make cheese that is buried in the ground while it ages. It is called 'formaggio di fossa', literally, 'cheese of the pit'. The cheese is made with sheep or cow's milk (or a combination of both). It is wrapped in muslin and buried in a straw-lined rocky pit – typically of volcanic ash – three to four metres (about three yards) deep, and matured for a period of up to three months. During this time the cheese develops a distinctive woody flavour.

The cheese vendor at the weekly market in Cervia encouraged me to have a taste; it was crumbly, pungent and intense – what I would have called a 'smelly cheese' as a child. These days this sort of cheese is right up my alley; a worthy companion to softer milder cheeses on a platter, and a sharp-tasting addition to gnocchi or risotto.

These gnocchi are a bit like gnudi; 'naked' filling for ravioli without their pasta coat. Adding the 'pit cheese' makes them more flavoursome, and works well if you add some bitter greens to the mix and coat them in melted butter at the end. I am lucky that my local specialised deli in Melbourne sells imported formaggio di fossa, but if you can't find it, use a crumbly strong-tasting sheep's milk cheese that has been aged no more than 12 months, such as pecorino sardo.

500 g (1 lb 2 oz) mixed greens (such as silverbeet/Swiss chard, spinach and witlof/chicory)

iced water, to refresh

200 g (7 oz) fresh ricotta, drained

100 g (3½ oz) parmesan, grated, plus extra to serve

100 g (3½ oz) formaggio di fossa or a crumbly pecorino, grated

2 eggs, lightly beaten

100 g (3½ oz/1 cup) dried breadcrumbs

1 teaspoon chopped dill

finely grated zest of ½ lemon

sea salt and freshly ground black pepper

100 g (3½ oz) unsalted butter

Bring a large saucepan of salted water to the boil. Wash and trim the greens, then plunge them into the boiling water. Once it comes to boil again, let the greens cook for a few minutes. Drain and refresh in iced water (to help retain their colour), then roughly chop and allow to cool.

Meanwhile, place the ricotta, grated cheeses and egg in a large bowl and stir until well combined. Add the cooled greens, breadcrumbs, dill, lemon zest and salt and pepper to taste and combine well – the mixture will be quite thick. Roll the mixture into walnut-sized balls. Ideally the gnocchi should be cooked as soon as you make them – don't let them rest too long.

Bring a large saucepan of water to the boil. Before you add the gnocchi to the water, melt the butter in a large deep frying pan over low heat. (You may need to do this in two pans or batches if you don't have a very large pan.) Once the water is at a rolling boil, carefully drop in the gnocchi in batches, using a slotted spoon. Once they rise to the surface, lift them out with the slotted spoon and carefully drop them into the melted butter. Allow the gnocchi to cook for a few minutes on each side until nicely golden. Spoon onto warmed serving places and drizzle over some of the deep-golden butter. Scatter with extra grated parmesan and serve immediately.

SERVES 4

Tagliatelle alle ortiche
Stinging nettle tagliatelle

Green stinging nettles are actually weeds. They often grow along fences, ditches and in fields, close to where animals are grazing. If you find them growing near you, consider yourself lucky as it means the soil is filled with nutrients. Their aromatic flavour and distinctive fragrance makes them a useful ingredient in the kitchen, in pesto, risotto, omelettes and soup. I add nettles to homemade egg pasta to make vibrant green tagliatelle. Just remember when handling nettles that they do sting, so use gloves. Once cooked, the stinging effect is removed so you can touch them without any prickly side-effects.

If you have any leftover nettles, you can blanch and drain them, then freeze them in an ice-cube tray for later use.

200 g (7 oz) stinging nettles,

400 g (14 oz) 00 flour or plain (all-purpose) flour

3 large eggs

superfine semolina (semola rimacinata), for dusting

180 g (6½ oz) unsalted butter, diced

24 sage leaves

finely grated zest of 1 lemon

sea salt and freshly ground black pepper

grated parmesan, to serve

Wearing gloves, pick the leaves and smaller stems from the nettles, discarding any thicker stems and damaged leaves. Wash in plenty of cold water and pat dry. You should have about 150 g (5½ oz) left. Plunge the nettles into a saucepan of boiling water, then drain the leaves in a colander. Rinse them in cold water and leave to cool, then wring them out with your hands (no gloves needed) and chop finely.

Follow the instructions on pages 22–23 for making egg pasta, dropping in the finely chopped nettles as you combine the flour and eggs. Depending on how wet the nettles are, you may need to add a dash of water or a bit more flour to achieve the right consistency. Cover and allow to rest for at least 30 minutes.

Make the tagliatelle by running the pasta through your pasta machine until it is the desired thickness (I took mine to the third last setting of my machine), using superfine semolina for dusting. Cut the dough using the tagliatelle attachment, then dust with more semolina and cover with a tea towel until you are ready to cook.

Cook the pasta in a large saucepan of salted boiling water for a few minutes until al dente.

While the pasta is cooking, melt the butter in a large frying pan over medium heat. Add the sage leaves and cook for a couple of minutes, just until they become fragrant.

Drain the pasta and place on a serving dish. Pour on the sage butter and sprinkle over the lemon zest, salt, pepper and plenty of grated parmesan.

SERVES 4

Stufato di cefalo
Fish and potato stew

The marshy waters that lie in the lowlands of Emilia-Romagna could be called 'acque di mezzo' (waters that lie between land and sea). They are home to varieties of seafood that can tolerate lower salt levels, such as squid, eel and mullet.

In his online recipe booklet Ricette di Cucina delle 'Acque di Mezzo' *Sandro Bignami describes some of the dishes of the lowlands, combining elements of the land and the sea. This recipe is taken from the book, slightly tweaked. It's one of those one-pot dishes that make cooking for a group so easy. Pancetta, onions and butter are slowly braised to make a well-seasoned base for baby potatoes and bites of tender fish. Serve from the pan at the table, adding a good sprinkling of parsley and spring onion (scallion) at the end.*

If you can't find mullet, trevally makes a good substitute.

40 g (1½ oz) butter

2 teaspoons extra virgin olive oil

60 g (2 oz) pancetta, finely diced

1 large brown onion,
finely diced

1 clove garlic, crushed

350 g (12 oz) small new
potatoes, halved

80 ml (2½ fl oz/⅓ cup)
tomato passata

500 g (1 lb 2 oz) mullet fillets,
skin and bones removed,
cut into bite-sized pieces

sea salt and freshly ground
black pepper

flat-leaf parsley leaves and sliced
spring onion (scallion),
to garnish

crusty bread, to serve

Place the butter and olive oil in a large frying pan over low heat. When the butter has melted, add the pancetta and cook for 5 minutes or until softened and starting to release its fat. Add the onion and cook gently for about 20 minutes until well softened but not coloured. Add the garlic and cook for a couple of minutes until fragrant, then add the potatoes, passata and 250 ml (8½ fl oz/1 cup) of water. Increase the heat and bring to the boil, then reduce to the heat to low and simmer, covered, for 15–20 minutes until the potatoes are just cooked through but still firm.

Add the fish and cook, covered, for another 10–15 minutes until cooked through. Remove the lid for the last 5 minutes or so if there is too much sauce. Season to taste with salt and pepper. Garnish with parsley and spring onion and serve with crusty bread to mop up the juices.

SERVES 4

Pesce in crosta di sale
Salt-crust fish

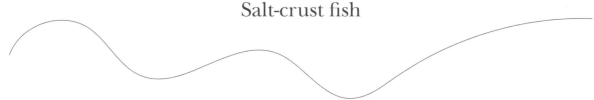

Burying a whole fish in salt is both simple and slightly nerve-wracking. The technique has been used for centuries and basically allows the fish to steam within its salty case, imparting a delicate seasoning to the flesh. The traditional way is to only use coarse salt, but I'm afraid I am not willing to risk a dreaded crack appearing as the fish cooks, which could potentially dry out the moist flesh. I add egg whites to help bind the salt casing. When the fish is cooked, there is nothing quite as dramatic as taking to the hard crust with a small mallet to make it crack, particularly if you have an audience.

Ask your fishmonger to clean the cavity of the fish but leave the scales intact; this will allow the salt crust to separate more easily from the skin once it is cooked. Make sure the fish is as close as possible to the recommended weight as otherwise you will need to adjust the cooking time. This dish is even better served with a side of smashed potatoes and greens (page 270) and a little flat-leaf parsley sauce (page 148).

1 x 1.2 kg (2 lb 10 oz) whole fish (snapper or sea bream)

½ lemon, cut into thick slices

a few flat-leaf parsley and dill sprigs, plus extra to serve

1.5 kg (3 lb 5 oz) coarse sea salt

5 egg whites

1 kg (2 lb 3 oz) fine sea salt

juice of 1–2 lemons

Preheat the oven to 180°C (350°F) and line a baking tray with baking paper, if you like.

Wash the fish and pat dry. Stuff the cavity with the lemon slices and herbs.

Place the coarse salt and egg whites in a food processor and whiz until it comes together. Transfer the mixture to a bowl, add the fine salt and mix well.

Place a 1 cm (½ in) thick layer of the salt mixture on the prepared tray in the approximate shape of the fish. Lay the fish on top and cover with the rest of the salt mixture, packing it against the fish. It is important that the fish is completely sealed within the crust.

Bake for 35 minutes (the rule of thumb is 30 minutes for every 1 kilogram/2 lb 3 oz of fish). Remove from the oven immediately and allow to rest for 10 minutes.

Crack open the crust and remove the skin. Drizzle over the lemon juice and scatter with extra parsley and dill to serve.

SERVES 4

Quaqlie in umido
Quail with pancetta, olives and Marsala

There are hundreds of species of birds in the park of the Po River valley, attracted to the rich landscape of forests and woods, wetlands and salt-water lagoons. Birds have always been a significant part of the local diet, often caught and simply roasted over the coals.

In place of the wild-caught birds of the past, farmed quail from speciality butchers can be used in this dish. I have made it with whole quail, but when it comes to eating them, some members of my family look at me with alarm. My mother will happily clean the bones of all the succulent meat, but she is the only one; the rest of us tend to pick at the small bird, leaving a good proportion of meat. So I have taken to quartering and semi-boning the birds to remove the visual cues and make eating them much easier. It takes a bit of practice but it's a service that many butchers will do for you anyway. My mother prefers the quail to remain whole, so it is all a matter of personal preference.

Make sure you serve the dish with bread or soft polenta to mop up the delicious juices.

6 quails (about 180 g/6½ oz each)

sea salt

2 tablespoons extra virgin olive oil

40 g (1½ oz) unsalted butter

50 g (1¾ oz) thickly cut smoked pancetta, diced

1 brown onion, finely diced

4 small fresh or dried bay leaves

¼ lemon, halved

90 g (3 oz) dried olives, halved and pitted

125 ml (4 fl oz/½ cup) Marsala

250 ml (8½ fl oz/1 cup) chicken stock, preferably homemade

sea salt and freshly ground black pepper

soft polenta (see page 14) or crusty bread, to serve

Remove the breastbones and cut each bird into four pieces: two thighs with the bone in and two breasts. If you do not want to cut the bird yourself, ask your butcher to do it for you. Wash the quail pieces and pat dry, then season with salt.

Place the olive oil and butter in a frying pan that is large enough to fit all the pieces of quail in a single layer and heat over medium–high heat. Once the butter has melted, add the quail pieces (in batches if needed) and sear for about 1 minute on each side, turning them over with tongs. They will brown quickly. Transfer to a baking dish and cover with foil to keep warm. Reduce the heat to medium, and scrape up any pieces of meat or skin stuck to the base of the pan, leaving them in the pan.

Add the pancetta, onion, bay leaves, lemon and olives to the pan and cook over medium–low heat, stirring occasionally, for 10 minutes or until the onion is translucent and the fat on the pancetta has rendered. Add the Marsala and turn up the heat. Let it bubble away for 3–4 minutes until most of the Marsala has evaporated, then add the chicken stock and reduce the heat to medium. Bring to a simmer, then return the quail pieces to the pan and reduce the heat to medium–low. Cover and cook for 8–10 minutes, then check the meat for readiness – it should be very tender and cooked through. Turn up the heat briefly if there is too much liquid in the pan to allow it to reduce slightly. Taste and add some salt and pepper if needed.

Serve with plenty of soft polenta or crusty bread.

SERVES 4

SALT
THE SWEET SALT OF CERVIA

I was in Ravenna for six days, and most of them were spent driving to and from the coast, past the reed-lined canals and fishing huts, watching flocks of birds dipping and diving from the sky to the lagoons in the distance. I was in search of salt, giant mountains of it – the sweet salt of Cervia. I had read that the mounds would appear on the horizon as I was driving along the Adriatica (the road that runs parallel to the Adriatic coast from the north to the south of Italy). I couldn't see any though, as I zig-zagged between the salt museum in the town of Cervia and the information centre. It was only when I was directed to the 'salina' (salt mine) that I saw the large grey crystalline pyramids straight ahead, just beyond a boom gate.

SALT

THE SWEET SALT OF CERVIA

In the days prior to refrigeration salt was essential for the preservation of food. Although there is less demand for salt now, in those days it was known as white gold. Without salt, meat couldn't be dried to make salami and prosciutto; sardines, anchovies and cod couldn't be salt preserved; there would be no cheese; and food would be bland. The word 'salary' comes from 'salt', as being paid in salt was, at one time, as good as being paid in cash. From the 1200s to the 1500s, the Republic of Venice controlled salt production and distribution in the Adriatic and part of the Mediterranean, and if they couldn't control a salt mine, they destroyed it. In the mid 1500s the Pope imposed a salt tax in central Italy, and there was a terrible war and salt shortage; the people of Tuscany and Umbria refused to pay the tax and, out of necessity, made their bread without salt. They continue to do so.

Letizia Magnani's 2015 account of the sweet salt of Cervia, *Dolce come il sale*, describes the history of salt in the area. It goes back to Etruscan times, when the old town of Cervia was right in the middle of the salt pans and was called Ficocle. The marshy and low-lying land encouraged the spread of malaria among the salt-workers, or 'salinari', who were frequently sick, and in the 1600s the people of Cervia implored the Pope to help them. Such was the importance of salt at that time that help arrived; the solution was to move the town itself, brick by brick, to a different location, closer to the coast and a short distance from the salt pans. 'Cervia Nuova', the new town of Cervia, was built in 1697 around a central 'canale delle saline', which was used to transport the salt from the mines to the storage warehouses. The new town was dedicated almost entirely to salt production, with workers' cottages, salt storage warehouses and a square fortress of sorts, the San Michele tower, to protect the precious 'white gold' from pirates who, up until the early 1800s, sailed the waters of the Adriatic Sea.

I joined a school group to tour both the salt pans and the salt mine. It was early spring and the salt production season had not yet started. The rectangular pans looked like shallow lakes and, walking along the grassy embankment, our tour guide pointed out one of the many flocks of stilt plovers across the water. He told us that in the warmer months, it is common to see flocks of pink flamingos that have in recent years made a home in the area. During the summer, when sea water is being concentrated in the pans to form salt, the rectangular pans are coloured shades of pink and grey, due to the presence of a tiny pink brine shrimp.

At the salt mine, I chatted to guides Elisa and Davide as we walked past the impressive salt pyramid with its crystalline hard grey surface. Elisa reminded the school children not to touch the grey mound, although I was also tempted to pat it ever so lightly to see what it felt like. Elisa explained that the pyramid represents the salt collection of an entire year. It is not all packaged at once; it is retrieved from the mound as needed.

The children asked why the salt just didn't wash away with the rain (a good question, I thought). Davide explained that the crust that forms is actually caused by the rain, which dissolves the outermost layer of the salt, crystallising it into a protective barrier for the remaining salt. The basic process for making sea salt is simple: salty water enters a shallow enclosed space and eventually the water evaporates in the sun, leaving a crystalline layer of salt where the water once was. The salt mines of Cervia, being in a more northerly position, only have one collection season per year, corresponding broadly to the summer (unlike those further south in Sicily where there are multiple collections each year).

Up until 1959 salt was collected traditionally. There were 144 basins with multiple troughs in Cervia. Sea water entered the basins, slowly evaporating and becoming more concentrated through a system of channels before finally ending up in basins called 'cavedini', where salt was formed. The salinari worked their own basin and its five troughs, collecting the heavy wet salt every day from April through to September. They used a wooden rake, scraping and collecting the salt that had formed in the first trough, then the next day they moved to the second trough, and so on. On day six the whole process started again from the first trough, a continual daily collection process for the season. Once the salt was collected, it was drained, piled high and transported to the salt warehouses in Cervia in iron boats along the central town canal. There it was washed, weighed, packaged and stored.

In 1959 the Italian government issued a directive to implement a new method of salt production, one that was more efficient and less costly. The small basins were joined into larger ones, and now there is a single massive annual collection by machine, a major change for those whose families have been salinari for generations. Only a few could be employed in the new salt factory and many moved on, several working towards establishing the museum and tourist facilities to tell the story of how it was in the old days.

There is now only one remaining salt pan that uses the old wooden tools in the traditional method: the Camillone, operating as a kind of open-air salt museum. The pink salt, heavy with sea water, is collected manually by rake about twice a week during summer. So what is it about this salt that makes it so special? All you need to do is taste a flake or granule and you'll see. (It only comes in two forms: either as a coarse salt or as 'salfiore', the first white crystals that are formed on the surface of the water, which are used as a finishing salt.) You will notice there is no bitter aftertaste that makes you reach for a glass of water. Have another, just to double check, and you will agree that compared with other salts, it is sweet. The relatively cooler climate of the more northern Adriatic ensures that there are very few bitter impurities; it is close to pure sodium chloride. It is also 'integrale' or whole, as it is washed with super-saturated water and then allowed to dry naturally.

Salt made the town of Cervia; everyone who lives there has a story to tell of their family connection to the salinari, and through it, their connection to each other. A walk through the town on Thursday, the day of the weekly market, sees a hive of activity around the old salt warehouses, tower San Michele and the canal: tent-like stalls selling fruit and vegetables on one side of the bridge crossing the canal, and clothing stalls and bric-a-brac on the other side. Fishing boats line the canale delle saline, fishermen cleaning their nets and hosing down their buckets. It seems like any other town, except for the imposing watch tower that dominates the canal, its adjacent red-brick salt warehouses on both sides of the canal, and the tour marker signs that dot the canal and adjacent streets, with photos that tell the stories of the sweet salt of Cervia.

Piadina zucca, patate e salsiccia
Bread pockets with pumpkin, potato and pork sausage

While driving on the road between Ravenna and Cervia we passed several small rivers with fishing huts on them. Along one of them was a food van, La vera piadina di Mirella. It was only 10 o'clock in the morning, but it was open and ready for business. A 'piadina' is a bread pocket and Mirella sold them filled with eggplant (aubergine) and porchetta; prosciutto and cheese; sausage, onion and capsicum, and even one filled with a chocolate–hazelnut spread. She warmed our chosen piadine, wrapped them in paper and we ate them, looking out at the fishing shacks.

Piadine are surprisingly easy to make at home. Discs of dough are filled and folded into a semi-circle, and then two piadine are cooked side by side in a large frying pan. When the bread is firm and pleasantly golden you need to carefully flip them over. The filling stays warm in the bread pocket for some time if covered loosely with foil, giving you enough time to cook a second lot of piadine. Experiment with other fillings – braised bitter greens, sausage and a sprinkling of chilli is also really nice.

300 g (10½ oz) potatoes, peeled and cut into large chunks

300 g (10½ oz) butternut pumpkin, peeled and cut into large chunks

olive oil, for pan-frying

250 g (9 oz) pork sausages, skins removed, broken into small chunks

50 g (1¾ oz) parmesan, grated

pinch of freshly grated nutmeg

sea salt and freshly ground black pepper

Dough

500 g (1 lb 2 oz) plain (all-purpose) flour

1 teaspoon salt

pinch of bicarbonate of soda (baking soda)

200 ml (7 fl oz) milk

125 ml (4 fl oz/½ cup) extra virgin olive oil

To make the dough, place the flour, salt and bicarbonate of soda in a large bowl and whisk to remove any lumps. Gradually add the milk and then the olive oil, mixing by hand as you go. Tip the dough onto a lightly floured work surface and knead for 5 minutes or until smooth. Cover and set aside for at least 30 minutes.

Place the potato in a saucepan of cold water. Bring to the boil, then reduce the heat and simmer for 10–20 minutes until fork-tender (the cooking time will depend on the size of the chunks). Drain and roughly mash. Repeat this process with the pumpkin, letting it drain well before you mash it.

Heat a splash of olive oil in a small frying pan over medium heat, add the sausage meat and cook for 7–8 minutes until cooked through. Set aside.

Combine the potato and pumpkin mash, parmesan and nutmeg in a bowl and season to taste with salt and pepper. Set aside.

Cut the dough into quarters. Roll out each piece to a 30 cm (12 in) circle, then cover each circle with a clean tea towel to prevent it from drying out.

Place a quarter of the potato mixture on one half of a dough circle, leaving a 1 cm (½ in) border. Scatter on a quarter of the sausage, then fold the other half of the dough over the filling, pressing the edges to seal or securing them with a fluted pastry wheel. Repeat with the remaining dough circles.

Heat a large non-stick frying pan with a lid over medium–high heat. Place two of the piadine in the pan, reduce the heat to medium–low and put the lid on. Check after 4–5 minutes – the underside should be nicely coloured and crisp; if not, leave it for another minute or two. Flip them over, then cover and cook for another 3–4 minutes. When the second side is cooked, use your tongs to lift the piadine and hold them upright in the pan for a few minutes to cook the folded edge. Transfer to a chopping board, and cover loosely with foil. Repeat with remaining piadine. Cut the pockets in half and serve warm.

MAKES 4

Asparagi in salsa
Asparagus with an egg sauce

To me, spears of green asparagus herald spring, and I love to have a constant supply in the fridge during the season. I mostly make risotto with it, but when there is only one person to cook for, I pair asparagus with eggs in an omelette (page 262) or simply enjoy it steamed with a vinaigrette dressing.

Another elegant way to have asparagus is with an eggy sauce. Mashing hard-boiled eggs might seem a bit 1970s, but adding anchovies, olive oil and parsley turns it into delightful sauce that I could easily eat spooned onto bread but also drizzle over lightly steamed asparagus. This recipe is very much like a dish I had in Ravenna not that long ago. Serve it as an accompaniment to barbecued bream (page 92) or baked anchovies with lemon (page 184), with a chilled glass of trebbiano.

750 g (1 lb 10 oz) thick green asparagus spears

3 hard-boiled eggs, peeled

2 anchovy fillets, chopped

juice of ½ lemon

80 ml (2½ fl oz/⅓ cup) mild extra virgin olive oil

sea salt and freshly ground black pepper

1 tablespoon finely chopped flat-leaf parsley, plus extra leaves to serve (optional)

Wash the asparagus spears and trim the woody ends. Steam the asparagus until just tender (a bit on the firm side is better). Set aside.

Meanwhile, remove the yolks from the hard-boiled eggs and place them in a small food processor (you won't need the egg whites). Add the chopped anchovy, lemon juice and olive oil and season to taste with salt and pepper (remembering the anchovies are quite salty). Blend until combined, then stir in the parsley. The sauce should be thick but pourable.

Arrange the steamed asparagus on a serving plate and spoon over the sauce. Finish with extra parsley, if you like, and a good grinding of black pepper.

SERVES 4

Ciambella alla Romagnola
Sweet log from Romagna

Although the word 'ciambella' usually refers to a cake with a hole in the middle, the Romagnoli like to shape their ciambella into a log. While visiting the town of Cervia I stopped in a pasticceria to have a mid-morning snack. There were trays of a long flattish yellow cake covered in thick granules of sugar – some were on sale and others were behind the counter. I asked the shop assistant what the cake was called and was told they were ciambella Romagnola. But why were some on sale? 'Oh, that one is from a few days ago, so it costs less. But I like it more than the fresh one – you slice it and dip it in wine, like you would with cantucci in Tuscany.'

So I took her advice and bought the older one; it was studded with sultanas and tasted of lemon zest. I had an open bottle of Sangiovese back at the apartment and dipped thick slices of the cake into the red wine. What a combination!

The ciambella is now on high rotation at home, but with woody pine nuts rather than sugar granules on the top. For me it's a ready-made breakfast or morning tea, usually dipped into milky coffee.

70 g (2½ oz) sultanas (golden raisins)

500 g (1 lb 2 oz) plain (all-purpose) flour

2 scant teaspoons baking powder

pinch of salt

3 eggs

170 g (6 oz) caster (superfine) sugar

60 g (2 oz) unsalted butter, melted and cooled

finely grated zest of 1 lemon

125 ml (4 fl oz/½ cup) milk

1½ tablespoons pine nuts

Place the sultanas in a bowl of hot water and soak for 30 minutes. Drain and set aside.

Preheat the oven to 180°C (350°F) and line a baking tray with baking paper.

Combine the flour, baking powder and salt in a bowl and whisk to remove any lumps.

Beat the eggs and sugar until light and fluffy. Add the flour mixture, butter, lemon zest, milk and drained sultanas and bring the ingredients together with a wooden spoon – it will be quite hard to mix. Tip the dough onto a lightly floured surface and, with floured hands, shape the dough into two even logs, about 20 cm (8 in) long and 7 cm (2¾ in) wide. Lift the logs onto the prepared tray, leaving plenty of room for spreading.

Sprinkle the pine nuts over the logs and bake for 30–35 minutes until golden and cooked through. Allow to cool completely before cutting into thick slices to serve. The ciambella will keep in an airtight container for up to a week.

MAKES TWO LOGS

Sabadoni
Chestnut and vincotto pastries

Ravioli come in all shapes, sizes and flavours, even sweet ones. You might like to think of 'sabadoni' as a type of sweet ravioli; pockets of barely-sweet dough are folded over and filled with a dense chestnut paste. They look a bit like an elaborate seashell. The parcels are baked and then, importantly, before serving they are soaked in vincotto for at least 15 minutes. The longer you let them infuse, the richer the taste of the sticky cooked grape must. They are quite dry otherwise, so this is an essential step.

If you can't find dried chestnuts, use whole cooked peeled ones from a tin. The recipe will need to be modified slightly though, so be sure you read the method carefully.

vincotto, for soaking

Filling

150 g (5½ oz) dried chestnuts (or 240 g/8½ oz tinned peeled whole cooked chestnuts)

250 ml (8½ fl oz/1 cup) milk

1 large strip orange peel (1 small strip if using tinned chestnuts)

25 g (1 oz/¼ cup) unsweetened dark cocoa powder

2 teaspoons caster (superfine) sugar

2 tablespoons apricot jam

finely grated zest of 1 orange

2 tablespoons vincotto

Pastry

250 g (9 oz) plain (all-purpose) flour

1 scant teaspoon baking powder

pinch of salt

30 g (1 oz) caster (superfine) sugar

125 g (4½ oz) chilled butter, cut into small cubes

3 eggs

2 tablespoons cold milk

To make the filling, soak the dried chestnuts in hot (not boiling) water for 1 hour. Drain, then place them in a small saucepan with the milk and orange peel. Bring to just below boiling point, then reduce the heat to low and simmer for 1 hour or more, checking periodically until they become soft, but still hold together. Leave to cool, then remove the orange peel. Place the chestnuts and any remaining milk in a food processor and whiz to form a stiff paste.

If you are using tinned chestnuts, drain them and put them in a blender with the smaller quantity of orange peel and only as much milk as you need to form a stiff paste.

Place the chestnut paste in a medium bowl and add the cocoa, sugar, apricot jam and orange zest. Mix to combine, then gradually add the vincotto, checking the consistency as you go. It should be quite stiff so you may not need all the vincotto.

To make the pastry, place the flour, baking powder, salt and sugar in a food processor and whiz briefly to combine. Drop in the butter, pulsing until the mixture resembles wet sand. Lastly add the eggs and half the milk and pulse until it comes together. If it does not come together, add the rest of the milk. Remove from the processor and, if needed, briefly knead until smooth.

Preheat the oven to 180°C (350°F). Line a large baking tray with baking paper.

Roll out the pastry to a thickness of 2 mm (¹⁄₁₆ in). I always roll pastry between two sheets of plastic film. Using a 9 cm (3½ in) round cutter, cut out about 24 circles. Place a heaped teaspoon of filling in the middle of each circle, then fold the dough into the centre in pleats, a little at a time, so each pleat is slightly overlapping. Arrange the sabadoni on the prepared tray, seam-side up (they should open up a bit as they cook).

Bake for 20–25 minutes until golden. Remove from the oven and cool completely on the tray. They will keep in an airtight container for several days. Before serving, soak them in vincotto for at least 15 minutes (up to an hour) so they can absorb some of the sweet liquid. Don't miss this step – it makes all the difference to the flavour and texture.

MAKES ABOUT 24

6

LA LAGUNA
VENETA

We caught a ferry from Rovinj, Croatia, and sailed across the Adriatic Sea to Venice. A water pathway for the boat was marked out in the Venetian Lagoon, bordered by wooden poles called 'bricole' arranged in groups of two or three. These serve to guide boats through deepened channels in the shallow waters to connect the larger islands. Birds cawed from above, perching on both the bricole and on the boat itself as we passed a few of the hundred or more islands of the lagoon. A few dozen are inhabited, but others are abandoned – former quarantine stations and asylums, brick walls in ruins and tangled overgrown gardens surrounded by marshes and reeds. There are still more that can hardly be called islands; instead they are mud flats or sand dunes that appear and disappear with time and tide.

With its exquisite palazzi, narrow canals and endless steps and bridges, the island of Venice never stops being thrilling, no matter how often you visit. Tens of thousands of people visit by day – meaning you are often jostling among them to visit the larger piazzas and churches and to stroll down the most popular 'calle' – only to leave it empty and quiet by night. Some locals have moved out to live in the surrounding areas or on the smaller islands, blaming the high cost of living and the high tides that frequently flood the lower levels of buildings. But to my visitor's eye it is beautiful, and a day or two spent there in the company of local resident and friend Enrica offered a journey through the glorious banquet days of the former Republic as well as an insight into the everyday life of the Venetians.

Enrica runs a cooking school and food is her passion. I bumped into her quite by chance last spring, sunning herself at an outdoor café in Dorsoduro. Between sips of espresso she asked me if I wanted see the market gardens on the islands. I immediately scrapped my other plans, because I knew that nothing would beat a day of island-hopping with Enrica. We caught a ferry to Punta Sabbioni and hired bicycles, Enrica's tiny dog Soia sitting happily in the basket at the front of hers. We rode along the flat roads that weave their way along the canals, eventually arriving at a couple of old farmhouses with large vegetable gardens. We walked around, down rows of artichokes and zucchini (courgettes) in the lee of hot houses of ripening tomatoes, past noisy chicken pens, and along fields of browning stems of garlic, soon to be picked. We stopped in a trattoria and ate 'botoi' (a type of baby artichoke) and 'moeche' (baby soft-shell crabs, stuffed with eggs and deep-fried), enjoying the seasonal tastes of Venetian spring cuisine. A bit later Livio, a friend of Enrica's called, offering us a ride back to Venice on his boat. After stopping on the island of Sant'Erasmo to buy some freshly picked green beans, we sailed into Venice, jostling for water space on the Grand Canal with gondolas, ferries and water taxis while Soia barked enthusiastically at the waves they made.

That night Enrica cooked us a Venetian feast in her elegant Dorsoduro apartment: peas and pancetta, asparagus salad, green beans and eggs, baby cuttlefish and capsicum, and a stuffed guinea fowl, all washed down with her own brand of prosecco.

As I made my way back to my accommodation later that night I felt truly fortunate. I had eaten a delectable feast cooked by a local, using the freshest of ingredients, and now I was walking through the empty streets of this magnificent city, dim lights illuminating narrow bridges on the same path that millions of people have walked along through the ages.

When I first met Enrica many years ago, one of the first places she took me was the Rialto market, right on the Grand Canal. It's a place I visit every time; I love the timelessness of the old market pavilion. Vendors joke with each other and occasionally hum a tune. Octopus, prawns and John Dory sit side by side on metal-framed benches at the historic fish market. Further along, under the red shades of the fruit and vegetable market, the long-haired artichoke seller deftly turns the large globes into disc-shaped 'fondi', dropping them in tubs of water with wedges of lemon to stop them from browning. Just beyond the markets, parched locals and tourists alike perch at one of the many 'bacari', enjoying a glass of wine and a snack – usually baccalà, eggs, anchovies or cured meats on a round of bread or a wedge of polenta.

As an outsider, I can't imagine life on the Venetian Lagoon is easy: the water and tides have always presented a challenge for growing food and obtaining supplies, though fish has always been plentiful of course. The lagoon's shallow sandy base, alternating with artificially deepened boating paths, tides and passages to the sea, mean that a wide variety of fish can be caught (and more recently, farmed) in this vast expanse of salt water. Bream, sea bass, sole, crabs, cuttlefish, scallops, clams, squid, calamari, mussels, mackerel, monkfish, anchovies – the list is long and varied.

On a visit to the colourful island of Burano and a walk along the shore of Rio Giudecca, you will see dozens of small fishing boats used by locals who fish the lagoon using traditional methods. I had a chat to one such fisherman, who was sitting in his boat busily brushing the shells of mussels he'd collected that morning. He told me he was going to give them to his daughter to cook for lunch; she didn't have time to clean them and he quite enjoyed being in the sun, scrubbing the shells clean with a wire brush. With the backdrop of yellow and pink houses and the quiet hum of everyday life, it seemed a world away from the elegant wigs, masks and carnival days of Venice.

Capesante gratinate
Oven-baked scallops

You will often see 'canestrelli' (queen scallops) in fish markets or restaurants on the islands of the Venetian Lagoon. They might look like miniature versions of regular scallops but they are actually a different variety, with a flat colourful fan-shaped shell. Sweet, delicate and so pretty, they are very popular in the northern Adriatic.

The easiest way to prepare plump, tender scallops is to top them with breadcrumbs and butter and bake them briefly at high temperature, shell and all. I often add a few extra toppings, such as finely chopped garlic, flat-leaf parsley and lemon zest, as a final touch. It seems stingy to only have one scallop per shell, especially if they are small, so I pile two or three on each fan-shaped shell. Afterwards I wash the shells, ready for next time I make the dish.

Here in Australia, canestrelli are not available so I substitute regular scallops. Remember that over-cooking scallops will make them tough and tasteless so be sure to use a timer.

36 small or 24 large scallops, ideally with the orange roe attached

12 scallop shells

1 clove garlic, finely chopped

3–4 tablespoons finely chopped flat-leaf parsley

35 g (1¼ oz/⅓ cup) dried breadcrumbs

50 g (1¾ oz) butter, at room temperature

finely grated zest of 1 lemon

sea salt

Preheat the oven to 220°C (430°F). Line a large baking tray with baking paper.

Wash the scallops and shells and pat dry. Arrange three small or two large scallops on each of the shells.

Mix together the garlic, parsley and breadcrumbs in a small bowl. Sprinkle the mixture over the scallops, then top evenly with butter.

Place them on the prepared tray and bake for 10 minutes until just firm and the breadcrumb topping is golden. Scatter on the lemon zest and sea salt to taste and serve immediately.

SERVES 4 AS A STARTER

Baccalà mantecato con crostini di polenta e prezzemolo
Whipped baccalà with polenta and flat-leaf parsley oil

Baccalà is salted cod (not to be confused with stockfish, which is dried cod) and was probably brought from Norway to Venice some time in the 1400s. It became very popular, both in Italy and Spain, due to its extended life and fleshy texture once reconstituted. In Venice, a popular way to eat baccalà is to whip it until it is creamy and smooth, and then spread it thickly on pieces of bread or firm polenta. There is a bit of a knack to the 'whipping' part. I use a small food processor and drizzle in the oil and milk a little bit at a time, stopping regularly to check the consistency. It should be spreadable and turn very white like whipped cream. You don't need to add any salt (it will be salty enough), and serving it with unsalted polenta and a herby parsley oil balances the whole thing out nicely.

I've recently discovered 'wet baccalà' which saves quite a bit of soaking time. You can find it in the deli section of larger Italian specialty food stores. It needs around 4 hours of soaking, changing the water a couple of times so the excess salt is removed. It should feel like firm fresh fish when it has soaked sufficiently. After soaking, remove the skin and any bones, leaving chunks of white flesh. If you can't find pre-soaked baccalà, you will have to increase the soaking time to up to 2 days, making sure you change the water at least every 12 hours.

300 g (10½ oz) wet baccalà

about 500 ml (17 fl oz/
2 cups) milk

1 clove garlic, crushed

90 ml (3 fl oz) mild extra virgin
olive oil

sea salt and freshly ground
black pepper

250 g (9 oz) instant polenta

2 tablespoons finely chopped
flat-leaf parsley

2 tablespoons extra virgin
olive oil

Place the wet baccalà in a large bowl of water and soak for 4 hours, changing the water two or three times. Taste a small piece of flesh; if it is still excessively salty, soak it a bit longer. It should still be salty, but edible. Drain.

Place the fish in a medium saucepan and cover with milk. The amount you use will depend on the size of your pan, but reserve about 90 ml (3 fl oz) of the milk for later. Slowly bring the milk to the boil and simmer for 30 minutes, then allow the fish to cool slightly in the milk.

Remove the fish and flake the pieces of flesh into chunks, discarding the skin and all bones, making sure you do not miss any small ones. You should have 250 g (9 oz) of flesh remaining; if you have more (or less) you may need to adjust how much milk and oil you add accordingly. Place the cleaned fish chunks and garlic in a food processor. Start processing and slowly pour in the mild olive oil, then the reserved milk, a little at a time, checking the consistency as you go and reducing or increasing the amounts you use depending on the weight of your fish. It should be white with a spreadable, mousse-like consistency. Taste and add salt and pepper (take care as you may not need salt); if it is still quite salty, don't add any salt to the polenta crostini (see below) and this should balance it out.

Pour 1 litre (34 fl oz/4 cups) of water into a medium–large saucepan and bring to a slow boil. Pour in the polenta in a steady stream, whisking the whole time to remove any lumps and reducing the heat as necessary so that it does not spatter. When it becomes very thick, swap the whisk for a wooden spoon and stir for a few more minutes or as per the instructions on your polenta packet. Spread the cooked polenta over a sheet of baking paper on a chopping board so it is about 1 cm (½ in) thick. Cover with another sheet of baking paper and roll out to an even thickness with a rolling pin (or use another board on top to flatten it). Allow to cool, then cut into squares or rectangles (mine were about 5 cm x 3 cm (2 in x 1¼ in).

While the polenta is cooling, mix together the parsley and olive oil.

Warm the polenta crostini by placing them briefly under a hot grill. Spoon the whipped baccalà on the crostini and drizzle with a little parsley oil just before serving.

The whipped baccalà will keep in an airtight container in the fridge for 4–5 days.

SERVES 8 AS AN APPETISER

Seppioline con peperoni
Baby cuttlefish with capsicum

Bite-sized 'moscardini' are a popular menu item that you often find in 'cicchetti' (snack) bars on the islands. Moscardini are a small type of octopus, with tiny grey tentacles that turn into pinkish curls once cooked. They need to be cooked slowly until they transform into the most tender of bites. This method works just as well with their cousins, 'seppioline' (baby cuttlefish) or 'calamaretti' (baby calamari). Go with what looks freshest at your local fishmonger on the day; they all need little cleaning, and are usually found already prepared. If you cannot find small cephalods, buy larger ones, clean them well (see page 16) and cut them into strips.

2 tablespoons extra virgin olive oil

1 clove garlic, peeled and left whole

500 g (1 lb 2 oz) baby cuttlefish, cleaned (see page 16) and patted dry

1 anchovy fillet, finely chopped

125 ml (4 fl oz/½ cup) dry white wine

2 red capsicums (peppers), seeds and membrane removed, cut into thin strips

200 g (7 oz) tinned peeled tomatoes

3 teaspoons white wine vinegar

freshly ground black pepper

1 tablespoon chopped flat-leaf parsley

crusty bread, to serve

Heat the olive oil in a large heavy-based saucepan over medium heat, add the garlic clove and warm it in the oil until fragrant. Add the baby cuttlefish and anchovy and cook for a few minutes, then increase the heat, add the wine and let it bubble away for 5 minutes or until the liquid has reduced a bit. Stir in the capsicum, tomatoes and vinegar.

Reduce the heat and simmer for 30–45 minutes until the cuttlefish and capsicum are fork-tender (the actual cooking time will depend on the size of the cuttlefish). Remove the garlic clove and season to taste with pepper. Scatter with parsley just before serving.

Serve warm or at room temperature with crusty bread to mop up the delicious sauce.

SERVES 4 AS AN APPETISER

Risi e verza
Cabbage risotto

Rice was introduced into Italian cooking from the East, probably arriving in northern Italy via Venice. It is a staple in the regions of Piedmont and Lombardy and widely used in the Veneto. Around the Venetian lagoons, simple dishes such as 'risi e bisi' (rice and peas) abound in spring. Somewhere between a soup and a risotto, it is traditionally made 'all'onda', meaning it is 'wavy' or 'runny', much like the waves on the sea (or on the lagoon when the boats pass).

A similar dish eaten in autumn is 'risi e verza' (rice and cabbage). Surprisingly sweet and velvety, the addition of butter and salty parmesan at the end of cooking produces a soupy risotto that is well balanced and delicious.

You can use vegetable stock to make this dish vegetarian, but I like the depth of flavour you get from using homemade chicken stock. I generally use everyday green cabbage but feel free to experiment with other varieties.

750 ml (25½ fl oz/3 cups) chicken stock, preferably homemade

2 tablespoons extra virgin olive oil

30 g (1 oz) unsalted butter

½ brown onion, finely diced

½ cabbage, thick spines removed, thinly sliced

1 clove garlic, peeled, bruised and left whole

200 g (7 oz/1 cup) carnaroli, vialone nano or arborio rice

sea salt and ground white pepper

50 g (1¾ oz) parmesan, grated, plus extra to serve

Pour the stock into a saucepan and bring to the boil. Reduce the heat and keep it simmering.

Heat the olive oil and butter in a large heavy-based saucepan over medium–low heat until the butter has melted. Add the onion, then reduce the heat to low and sauté for about 7 minutes until soft and translucent. Add the cabbage and garlic clove and stir well, then add about 125 ml (4 fl oz/½ cup) of the hot stock. Cover and cook for about 20 minutes until the cabbage has softened, stirring occasionally so the cabbage doesn't stick to the base.

Add the rice to the pan and stir so the rice warms through and is coated with the buttery cabbage. Add a ladleful of hot stock and stir well, allowing the rice to absorb the liquid. When all the liquid has been absorbed, add another ladleful of stock and continue cooking the rice as described – you want to keep it quite soupy. Continue cooking for about 20 minutes, adding stock as needed (or boiling water if you run out of stock) until the rice is cooked but still has a bit of bite. Remove the pan from the heat, add salt and pepper to taste, and remove the garlic clove (if you can find it!). Stir in the grated parmesan, then cover and let the risotto rest for a few minutes.

Serve on warmed plates, with extra parmesan on the side.

SERVES 4

Risotto agli asparagi bianchi e pancetta
Risotto with white asparagus and pancetta

My mother is Veneta, so if we weren't eating polenta we were eating risotto. I grew up eating it at least once, if not twice a week. She would make it with anything, often with leftovers such as her meat sugo or mushrooms cooked with garlic and white wine. All delicious, but one of my favourites was asparagus risotto as it heralded spring and the start of warmer weather. Back then we couldn't find white asparagus in Australia, although mamma would talk about it often, describing how she would eat it back in Italy. White asparagus is grown underground, in the dark; the absence of light means that it is unable to develop chlorophyll, which gives asparagus its green colour. These days white asparagus is readily available at good markets and greengrocers, but if you can't find the delicately flavoured white variety feel free to use its green cousin.

When you dice the pancetta, don't be tempted to remove the fattier part; the fat melts when the pancetta is heating, and these wonderful oils will later infuse the rice. It adds a depth of flavour that really makes the dish.

8 thick spears white asparagus

500 ml (17 fl oz/2 cups) vegetable stock, preferably homemade

1 tablespoon extra virgin olive oil

80 g (2¾ oz) pancetta, finely diced

200 g (7 oz/1 cup) carnaroli, vialone nano or arborio rice

25 g (1 oz) unsalted butter

sea salt and freshly ground black pepper

50 g (1¾ oz) parmesan, grated, plus extra to serve

1 teaspoon finely chopped flat-leaf parsley (optional)

Wash the asparagus spears and trim the woody ends. Cut the spears into 2 cm (¾ in) lengths; leave the tips a bit longer (about 3 cm/1¼ in) and keep them separate. Pour 250 ml (8½ fl oz/1 cup) of water into a small saucepan and bring to the boil. Drop in the shorter lengths of asparagus and cook for 4–5 minutes, then add the tips and cook for another 5 minutes. Drain, reserving all the water, and set aside.

Pour the stock and reserved water from the asparagus into a saucepan and bring to the boil. Reduce the heat and keep it simmering.

Heat the olive oil in a large heavy-based saucepan over medium–low heat, add the pancetta and cook for 4–5 minutes until the fat starts to be released (don't let it brown). Add the rice and stir so the rice warms through and is coated with oil. Add a ladleful of hot stock and stir well, allowing the rice to absorb the liquid. When all the liquid has been absorbed, add another ladleful of stock and continue cooking the rice as described – you want to keep it quite soupy. Continue cooking for about 10 minutes, then add the asparagus. Cook, adding stock as needed (or boiling water if you run out of stock) for another 8 minutes or until the rice is cooked but still has a bit of bite. Add the butter and let it melt, then stir it through. Remove the pan from the heat, add salt and pepper to taste and stir in the grated parmesan, then cover and let the risotto rest for a few minutes.

Serve on warmed plates, scattered with parsley (if using) and extra parmesan.

SERVES 4

Bigoli in salsa
Thick spaghetti with onions and anchovies

My parents and their friends used to get together for Italian card nights, which often finished up with singing. One of the songs, sung in our Venetian dialect, went something like this: 'me piase i bigoli co le luganighe Marieta damele per carità' (I like spaghetti with sausages, please give them to me Marietta). Every time we make 'bigoli in salsa', we start to sing this song. Well at least I do, often holding a glass of wine, like they did at those card nights, as I stir the sweet onions that make the sauce.

Rather than just being spaghetti, bigoli are traditionally a thick extruded pasta made with buckwheat or wholewheat flour. Although my parents might have served them with sausages, the Venetians serve them in a sauce of slowly cooked onions and anchovies. I like to balance the sweetness and saltiness of the two key ingredients by adding white wine vinegar or balsamic vinegar at the last minute. Feel free to experiment with the types of vinegar and how much to add; it really depends on your palate.

I like to make my own style of bigoli, and cut thick sheets of wholewheat pasta with an Abruzzese chitarra. If you don't want to make your own pasta, use store-bought thick pasta, preferably wholewheat.

80 ml (2½ fl oz/⅓ cup) extra virgin olive oil

2 large brown onions, very thinly sliced on a mandoline

12 anchovy fillets, finely chopped, plus extra fillets to serve (optional)

1 teaspoon balsamic vinegar (or to taste)

freshly ground black pepper

1 tablespoon finely chopped flat-leaf parsley

Pasta

200 g (7 oz) wholewheat flour

200 g (7 oz) superfine semolina (semola rimacinata), plus extra for dusting

2 eggs

To make the pasta, follow the instructions on pages 22–23 for making egg pasta, adding 100–120 ml (3½–4 fl oz) of water as you combine the flour and eggs. Cover and allow to rest for at least 30 minutes.

Cut the dough into quarters. Working with one portion at a time, roll it out on a surface that has been lightly dusted with superfine semolina. You can use a pasta machine or rolling pin to roll it to a 3 mm (⅛ in) thickness. Place the rectangle of dough on the narrower strings of the chitarra and, using a rolling pin, press on the dough so that the metal strings cut it into strips. Dust the prepared pasta with superfine semolina and cover with a clean tea towel to prevent it from drying out. Repeat with the remaining dough. If you don't have a chitarra, dust the pasta with superfine semolina, then loosely roll it up and cut it into 3 mm (⅛ in) wide strips with a knife.

Heat the olive oil and onion in a medium–large frying pan over medium–low heat, stirring frequently. The onion needs to cook slowly until it is translucent and starting to fall apart. It should not brown; reduce the heat if it starts to do this. After 15 minutes, add the anchovy to the onion and continue to cook for another 15 minutes or so. At the last minute, add balsamic vinegar and pepper to taste.

Place a large saucepan of salted water to the boil (don't add too much salt as the sauce can be quite salty). Drop in the pasta and cook until al dente (the cooking time will vary, depending on the thickness of the pasta). Drain, reserving a little of the pasta water in a cup. Add the pasta to the sauce and stir it well to coat. It should be a wet but dense sauce, so add some of the reserved cooking water if it looks a bit dry.

Serve on warmed plates, topped with parsley and extra anchovy fillets, if you like.

SERVES 4

Ravioli con asparagi, taleggio e noci
Ravioli with asparagus, taleggio and walnuts

I was enjoying a spring lunch with friends in Venice at a restaurant close to the Arsenale, and one of the dishes on the menu was ravioli with an asparagus filling. The asparagus had been grown on an island in the Venetian lagoon, Sant'Erasmo. The spears had been pulsed into a creamy green filling for the ravioli, which were doused with a piquant sauce made with taleggio cheese, then topped with flaked almonds. I rather liked the idea of recreating these at home, although I didn't make notes at the time so I only had a grainy photo to go on.

So this is what I came up with back home in winter: seasonal walnuts instead of almonds, which I pulsed to make a thick sauce with the taleggio, milk and butter. The asparagus filling is simpler and probably truer to the one I ate in Venice, with just cheese and asparagus. Judging by the speed at which my husband wolfed down the result I think I can consider my experiment a success. The white truffle oil is my friend Verdiana's suggestion. She is from Umbria so the flavour might not be typical of the Venetian Lagoon, so I have added it as an optional extra (albeit a highly recommended one).

400 g (14 oz) asparagus

iced water, for refreshing

150 g (5½ oz) taleggio,
roughly chopped

65 g (2¼ oz) parmesan, grated,
plus extra to serve

1 tablespoon finely chopped
flat-leaf parsley

80 ml (2½ fl oz/⅓ cup) milk,
plus extra if needed

40 g (1½ oz) butter

90 g (3 oz) walnuts

sea salt and freshly ground
black pepper

freshly grated nutmeg, to serve

white truffle oil, to serve
(optional)

Pasta

300 g (10½ oz) 00 flour or
plain (all-purpose) flour

3 eggs

superfine semolina
(semola rimacinata),
for dusting

To make the pasta, follow the instructions on pages 22–23 for making egg pasta. Cover and allow to rest for at least 30 minutes.

Meanwhile, wash the asparagus spears and trim the woody ends. Blanch in boiling water until just tender, then remove and refresh in iced water. Weigh out 250 g (9 oz) of asparagus and roughly chop it, then place in a small food processor (save the rest for later). Add 90 g (3 oz) of the taleggio, 45 g (1½ oz) of the parmesan, and the parsley and pulse to make a thick but chunky paste. Set aside.

Dust your work surface with superfine semolina. Cut the pasta dough in half. Working with one portion at a time, use a pasta machine to roll out the dough until it is quite thin (I took mine to the third last setting of my machine).

Place teaspoons of filling in a line on one edge of a sheet of pasta. Wet your finger with a bit of water and gently run it around the filling, then fold over the pasta sheet so that the mounds of filling are covered. Press down lightly to seal, making sure you have not incorporated any air. Cut the ravioli using a round or square mould, a fluted pastry cutter or even a knife (I used a 2.5 cm/1 in round ravioli cutter). Dust the prepared ravioli with semolina and cover with a clean tea towel, then repeat with the remaining pasta sheet and filling. You should make about 40–50 ravioli.

Combine the milk, butter and remaining taleggio and parmesan in a small saucepan over medium heat. When it all starts to melt stir well to combine, then remove from the heat. Allow to cool slightly and place in a mini food processor, along with 80 g (2¾ oz) of the walnuts. Pulse until a thick but pourable cream forms. Add a dash more milk if it is too thick. Season to taste with salt and pepper.

Crush the remaining walnuts and thinly slice the remaining blanched asparagus spears lengthways.

Place a large saucepan of salted water to the boil. Drop in the ravioli and cook for 4–5 minutes until al dente (the cooking time will vary, depending on the thickness of the pasta and the size of the ravioli). Drain well.

Place the ravioli on warmed plates and drizzle on the sauce. Scatter on the crushed walnuts, freshly grated nutmeg and extra parmesan, then garnish with the reserved sliced asparagus. Finish with a few drops of white truffle oil (if using) and serve immediately.

SERVES 4 AS A STARTER

Intingolo di coda di rospo
Monkfish stew

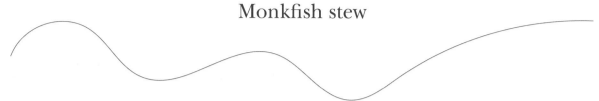

Monkfish isn't the prettiest fish to look at, with its large wide head and broad mouth full of tiny sharp teeth. In the water it can conceal itself from unsuspecting prey as it has seaweed-like appendages hanging from its body, enabling it to blend in with the underwater flora. It sounds like a nasty creature in the wild but it's a tasty one in the kitchen.

Monkfish flesh is sweet, meaty and quite similar to lobster. And if you can get the head from your fishmonger, all the better; it will make your sauce richer and more robust. In this recipe the fish head is bathed in olive oil, wine and tomato, then cooked with vegetables and herbs until it releases its flavour into the sauce, which is strained. Chunks of fish are then stewed in the rich red sauce until tender and served on soft yellow polenta.

Monkfish are native to the northern hemisphere, so if you are in the southern hemisphere, use stargazer or snapper. Your local fishmonger should be able to recommend the right substitution if you are unsure.

500 g (1 lb 2 oz) monkfish (with the head if possible)

3 tablespoons extra virgin olive oil

1 small carrot, peeled and roughly chopped

1 celery stalk, roughly chopped

½ brown onion, roughly chopped

125 ml (4 fl oz/½ cup) white wine

1 x 400 g (14 oz) tin whole peeled tomatoes

1 rosemary sprig

1 fresh or dried bay leaf

2 sage leaves

soft polenta (see page 14), to serve

2 tablespoons chopped flat-leaf parsley

Prepare the monkfish by separating the head from the body. You will be using the head to make the sauce and adding the pieces of fish later.

Heat the olive oil in a heavy-based saucepan over low heat, add the fish head, carrot, celery and onion and cook for about 5 minutes. Increase the heat to high, add the wine and let it bubble away until it has reduced. Reduce the heat to low and add the tomatoes and their liquid. Break up the tomatoes with a wooden spoon, then add the rosemary, bay and sage leaves and simmer, covered, for about 45 minutes.

Meanwhile, carefully remove the skin and bones from the monkfish and cut the flesh into bite-sized chunks.

Remove the fish head, vegetables and herbs from the sauce, and strain it through a wide-mesh strainer if needed. Place the fish pieces in the sauce and cook over low heat for 10–15 minutes until the fish has cooked through.

Serve on soft polenta, finished with a scattering of parsley.

SERVES 4

THE FOOD BOWL
OF THE VENETIAN LAGOON

Looking out from Fondamente Nove towards the islands of the northern part of the Venetian Lagoon, you will see a constant stream of boats and ferries, carrying people and supplies along the channel between Venice and the cemetery island of San Michele. If you are in luck, you might spy a blue-bottomed barge with colourful crates full of fresh produce: asparagus, beans, artichokes and zucchini (courgettes), collected from one of the islands that supply the markets and restaurants in Venice. Sant'Erasmo, Torcello, Vignole and Mazzorbo are not major tourist attractions when compared to the islands of Murano and Burano. They are sparsely populated and seldom visited, but they are the green spaces of the lagoon.

THE FOOD BOWL
OF THE VENETIAN LAGOON

As we skirted Sant'Erasmo by ferry, I could see patches of green, the occasional terracotta-coloured farmhouse and steps leading to candy-striped boat moorings on the canal. I got off the ferry at the second island stop, the one by the church, together with a handful of others. Most of them went into the church for the service, and I was completely alone: no shops, no crowds and, apart from the singing in the church, no sound except for the occasional lapping of water against the pier and the squawking of gulls overhead. I headed down the main road, with fields of artichokes peppered with red poppies on one side and endless rows of vines on the other. Over the water I could see other lagoon islands and distant boats. It was so close to the hubbub of Venice, but a world away.

Together with those on Vignole, the market gardens of the island of Sant'Erasmo supply their produce to the markets and restaurants of Venice. The gardens are mostly run by families, quietly going about the business of running a vegetable-producing farm in a most unusual location. The island produce is highly regarded; the particular environmental conditions and geographic location impart a taste and quality that is difficult to replicate in market gardens elsewhere. Apart from being surrounded by salt water, the islands occasionally flood, so the soil itself is a salty mixture of clay and sand, which imparts a delicate flavour to the fruit and vegetables that grow there.

One of the most sought-after vegetables is the small purple-violet artichoke of Sant'Erasmo. Artichoke season starts in mid spring, when 'castraure' (the small highly prized fleshy fruit that grow at the top of the plant) appear. Cutting the castraure encourages the plant to thrive and produce more artichokes known as 'botoi', which are slightly larger but almost as tasty. Castraure are sweet and tender, without a trace of bitterness, and they can be eaten raw.

A few weeks later when I was in Trieste, some 200 kilometres (125 miles) away, I had an itch to eat some of these artichokes before the season ended. After 90 minutes on the train and the tourist walk from the station to the Rialto market I found what I was looking for. Sadly there were no castraure, but I managed to find a dozen purple botoi. I'd met the vendor before, and when I told him that I'd travelled all the way from Trieste to buy Sant'Erasmo artichokes he laughed and gave me a couple extra, along with a big bunch of flat-leaf parsley.

A little-known fact is that grape vines grow on the islands in the Venetian Lagoon. On Venice itself in the area of Castello there is a church called San Francesco della Vigna, or St Francis of the Vineyard. Around 1250 the Doge gave a group of Franciscan monks a piece of land with vines on it. Vineyards, as well as orchards and gardens, were often managed by monks so are often found adjacent to churches. In my research I'd heard that there was a vineyard adjacent to the Basilica of Santa Maria Assunta on Torcello, the island that some call the predecessor to Venice. In the late 1400s people moved to other islands on the lagoon, abandoning Torcello because of disease and a build-up of silt in the canals. It became a predominantly green space with only a few buildings and even fewer people.

I arrived at Torcello by ferry, a much smaller boat than the ones that take the crowds to the other islands. A handful of people got off and seemed to know where to go – not that there was much choice as there was a single path along a canal, past green fields to a cluster of buildings. Cipriani, the restaurant famous for its many illustrious guests including Ernest Hemingway, was closed so I walked towards what seemed like the last arrival point of the path: the Basilica of Santa Maria Assunta and its adjacent belltower. For a small fee you can climb the many stairs to the top of the tower. It is well worth it as the views are breathtaking: canals snaking through patches of green on one side, fields of vegetables on another, and on yet another, a view of the pink and blue houses of Burano in the distance, across an expanse of blue water.

The tiny vineyard is right next to the Basilica; it has rows of vines alternating with statue-lined paths, and a wide canal just beyond. There were once other vineyards on the islands, some dating back to Roman times, but most were lost in the floods of 1966, the worst in the history of the lagoon. Many were abandoned because of the damage caused by flood waters: the high level of salinity was disastrous for the vines.

One of the most fascinating tales of the lost vines of the lagoon is the story of the winery Venissa, on the island of Mazzorbo. If you take a short stroll from the colourful island of Burano, over a bridge and onto Mazzorbo, you can reach the enclosed garden of Venissa, with its rows of vines and flowering red and pink roses. The belltower of the former Monastery of Sant'Eufemia looks over the grounds, onto statues, artichoke plants and herbs, a pond and a restaurant.

The story of Venissa is the story of Dorona, a white grape native to the Venetian islands, all but lost after the 1966 floods. Matteo Bisol, son of owner Gianluca, told me some of the story when I had lunch at the Venissa restaurant. Gianluca was visiting Torcello in 2001 and he noticed the vineyard next to the Basilica, which he had not seen before. While walking through the vines he noticed three plants of an old Venetian grape varietal that he had never encountered. It was Dorona. He researched and found out that this white grape is native to the islands of Venice and was once common, but was thought to be lost after the 1966 floods. Gianluca then managed to find some remnant Dorona vines surviving on one of the adjacent islands. He planted them in the former vineyard of the Monastery of Sant'Eufemia on Mazzorbo, which had also been abandoned since the terrible flood. The vines thrived and the first vintage was in 2010.

We had a beautiful meal at Venissa and shared a glass of Dorona. The salty environment gives the wine a strong minerality and a syrupy gold colour. It is made and aged in a way that is more in line with red wine, giving it a robustness that it not often found in a white. The bottles in which the wine is sold add to the story; they are made on nearby Burano and are decorated with hand-beaten gold leaf, an ideal fit with the name of the grape, 'Dorona' (similar to 'd'oro', meaning 'of gold').

Faraona ripiena
Stuffed guinea fowl

My Venetian friend Enrica loves cooking guinea fowl at her home in Dorsoduro for special occasions. She described a chestnut and pork sausage stuffing to me as we ate a few snacks at her favourite bar near the Rialto, all'Arco. 'Don't forget to wrap the bird in pancetta or else it will dry out,' she advised me between sips of prosecco.

The wrapping part is easier said than done - using narrow slices of flat pancetta is quite messy. Larger slices make it easier, and adding prunes and some finely chopped mushrooms adds a sweet earthiness to the stuffing.

The bird does look quite inelegant as it cooks, as its legs can splay in all directions. If this bothers you, you can truss the bird, although I usually don't. The seasoned pan juices are for drizzling on the cooked bird, but when I made this I couldn't resist mopping them up with bread.

1 guinea fowl (about 1 kg/
2 lb 3 oz), cleaned

50 g (1¾ oz) crustless bread,
broken into pieces

125 ml (4 fl oz/½ cup) milk

1 pure pork sausage

3 soft prunes, pitted and
chopped

50 g (1¾ oz) brown mushrooms,
finely chopped

1 small egg

25 g (1 oz) parmesan, grated

2 small sage leaves, chopped

sea salt and freshly ground
black pepper

3 tablespoons extra virgin
olive oil

¼ large lemon, skin removed,
cut into 4 segments

150 g (5½ oz) prosciutto,
thinly sliced

crusty bread, to serve (optional)

Preheat the oven to 200°C (400°F) and oil a roasting tin.

Wash the bird inside and out and pat dry.

Soak the bread in the milk for a few minutes. Squeeze and set aside.

Remove the skin from the sausage and break the meat into pieces. Place in a bowl with the soaked bread, prunes, mushrooms, egg, parmesan and sage, season to taste with salt and pepper and mix with a wooden spoon or your hands until well combined.

Sprinkle a bit of salt on the bird and massage it into the skin. Fill the guinea fowl with the stuffing (you might have some left over, depending on the size of the bird) and secure the opening with toothpicks. Rub 2 tablespoons of olive oil over the bird, and place the lemon segments under the wings and legs (in the fold where the wings and legs touch the body). Wrap the body of the bird in prosciutto so it is completely covered. This will prevent it from drying out in the oven.

Rub a large sheet of foil with the remaining olive oil, then wrap the bird in it. Place it in the prepared tin and bake for 1 hour. Open up the foil and bake for a further 30 minutes. Test whether the bird is cooked through by piercing the flesh with a metal skewer – any juices that run out should be clear. Cover and rest for 15 minutes before serving.

Using a large knife or kitchen scissors, cut the bird into about 12 pieces. Serve drizzled with pan juices, with bread to mop them up (if you like).

SERVES 6

Carciofini lessi
Baby artichoke salad

Last spring I sat in a café on the island of Sant'Erasmo, sipping white wine and looking out over the lagoon. The café was quite modest but the menu seemed very good. The first item was 'botoli lessi' (boiled baby artichokes), to be ordered individually. I ordered three. Then I ordered another two. Then I was tempted to cancel main course and order another five. They were just warm, lightly salted but sweet, and they melted in my mouth; unquestionably the best artichokes I had ever eaten and made all the more special with an enviable lagoon view.

Making this dish at home is not easy – for a start, most of us are nowhere near Venice. Botoi or botoli cannot be easily substituted with other artichokes because of the inherent saltiness they have from growing on a lagoon island. However, you can get a close approximation by using young, tender elongated artichokes (not the ball-like globe variety). Ask your local greengrocer if he or she can source some for you. Ideally the artichokes should have at least a few centimetres (about an inch) of stem as this part is delicious – some say the best part.

You won't need to remove the hairy choke at the centre because small artichokes shouldn't have them, but if you have only been able to find larger artichokes, you will need to do this. Follow the instructions in the recipe.

1 lemon

20 carciofini (botoli) from Sant'Erasmo (or other elongated baby artichokes)

125 ml (4 fl oz/½ cup) dry white wine, plus extra if needed

1 tablespoon extra virgin olive oil, plus extra to serve

sea salt

2 teaspoons finely chopped flat-leaf parsley

Half-fill a large bowl with water, squeeze the juice of the lemon into it and drop in one of the lemon halves. Using a sharp knife, cut off the tip of an artichoke flower (about a third of it) and chop off the lower dark part of the stem. Remove the outer leaves of the flower and slice off the outer part of the stem, rubbing the cut surface with the other lemon half as you go. If you have larger artichokes, you will need to halve (or even quarter) them vertically through the flower and scoop out the hairy choke using a small teaspoon. Repeat with the remaining artichokes, then leave them in the acidulated water for 30–60 minutes to remove any bitterness.

Select a large saucepan that will fit all the artichokes comfortably. Add the olive oil, then drop in the drained artichokes and cover with the wine and an equal quantity of water. Add more wine and water if needed – the amount required will depend on the size of the pan but you want them completely covered. Add salt to taste (you can always add a bit more later so don't add too much). Bring to the boil, then reduce the heat and simmer for 15–20 minutes until the artichokes are fork-tender.

Serve warm or at room temperature, topped with chopped parsley, sea salt to taste and a final drizzle of extra virgin olive oil.

SERVES 4 AS AN APPETISER

Torta di mele
Venetian apple cake

Most families on the islands in the lagoon have a recipe for apple cake their nonna or grandmother used to make – simple recipes that can be whipped up in a short amount of time, using pantry ingredients and apples, which are available most of the year.

I generally use tart apples when making cakes as I find the tartness balances all the sugar you add. Granny smiths are my favourites, though fuji or pink lady will also do. The addition of cinnamon to the top of the cake is a personal thing – my mother would never have dreamed of using it on her apple cakes as my father had an aversion to it. He used to say in half-Italian half-English 'non usar quella bloody cannella' ('Don't use that bloody cinnamon'), where 'bloody' was pronounced more like 'blah-di'. I leave the decision entirely up to you.

4 tart apples

juice of 1 small lemon

3 eggs

150 g (5½ oz) caster (superfine) sugar, plus 2 teaspoons extra

150 g (5½ oz/1 cup) plain (all-purpose) flour

30 g (1 oz) cornflour (cornstarch)

1 scant teaspoon baking powder

pinch of salt

80 g (2¾ oz) unsalted butter, softened

1 teaspoon vanilla essence

1 teaspoon ground cinnamon

Preheat the oven to 180°C (350°F). Line the base and side of a 23 cm (9 in) cake tin with a removable base.

Peel and core the apples and cut them into quarters, then cut each quarter into four or five slices, depending on how big the apple is. Place in a bowl, add the lemon juice and toss so the slices are coated (this will help stop them going brown). Set aside while you prepare the batter.

Beat the eggs and sugar with an electric mixer until the mixture is pale and fluffy. Place the flours, baking powder and salt in a bowl and whisk briefly. Fold the dry ingredients into the egg mixture until well incorporated, then add the butter and vanilla and fold until well combined.

Divide the apple slices into two portions: one of about 250 g (9 oz) and the other of about 150 g (5½ oz). Cut the larger portion of apple slices in half, then fold them into the batter, including any juice from the bowl. Leave the remaining 150 g (5½ oz) apple slices uncut and set them aside.

Spoon the batter into the prepared tin and smooth the surface. Arrange the remaining apple slices in a circular pattern on top of the cake, pressing them down gently so they partially sink into the batter. Sprinkle the top with the cinnamon and the extra sugar.

Bake for 50 minutes or until the top of the cake is golden and a skewer inserted in the middle comes out clean. Serve warm or at room temperature.

SERVES 10–12

Bussolai
Venetian s-shaped biscuits

A Tola co i Nostri Veci (At the Table with Our Old Folk) by Mariù Salvatori de Zuliani is a cookbook entirely written in Venetian dialect. It has hundreds of old and sometimes forgotten recipes, often with scant detail. It describes how 'bussolai' (also known as bussolari) were originally made with bread dough and shaped like a ring. They were dry, crisp and used in place of bread, either to accompany a meal or for dipping in milky coffee for breakfast.

It seems that later a sweet version came about, again ring-shaped, with variations including the addition of butter, almonds and liqueur. However, the s-shape makes it easier to dip the whole buttery biscuit in a goblet of wine, which I often do.

3 egg yolks

90 g (3 oz) caster (superfine) sugar

100 g (3½ oz) unsalted butter, at room temperature

250 g (9 oz/1⅔ cups) plain (all-purpose) flour

pinch of salt

finely grated zest of 1 lemon

finely grated zest of ½ orange

1 vanilla bean, split lengthways and seeds scraped

Beat the eggs and sugar with an electric mixer until the mixture is pale and fluffy. Add the butter and beat until well combined. Add the flour, salt, lemon and orange zest and vanilla seeds, and mix with a spoon and then your hands until well incorporated. Wrap the dough in plastic film and let it rest in the fridge for at least 1 hour.

Preheat the oven to 170°C (340°F). Line a large baking tray with baking paper.

Using about 30 g (1 oz) of dough per biscuit, form the dough into 10 cm (4 in) logs and bend them into an s-shape. Place them on the prepared tray and bake for 15–17 minutes until they are golden underneath but still pale on top. Cool completely on the tray before eating.

The biscuits will keep in an airtight container for several weeks.

MAKES 16–18

7

IL GOLFO DI TRIESTE

At the most northern point of the Adriatic Sea sits the port town of Trieste, an elegant and grand city that looks quite a bit like Vienna. It was in fact part of Austria for hundreds of years, and prior to that part of the Republic of Venice. With its rocky 'Carso' to the north, leading into mountainous Friuli, and Slovenia only a stone's throw away, it is a unique marriage of diverse cultures, reflected in the language spoken in the local townships, in the people themselves and, of course, in the food.

Unsurprisingly, the cuisine of the area that spills into the Gulf of Trieste is dominated by fish, courtesy of its Venetian history and location, but also by pork and potatoes from its more recent Austro-Hungarian occupation and the pockets of Slovenians who live in the province. One of the most common and best-loved winter soups in trattorias and on family tables is 'iota' or 'jota', a soup made with dried beans, flavoured with speck or ham bones and blended with sauerkraut. You also see goulash on menu boards in most traditional restaurants, served with pasta or potatoes, and if you are close to the coast it's not uncommon for farmers to make their own prosciutto and sausages.

There is a thriving fishing trade in Trieste and the other nearby coastal towns, where the waters are shallow and fish such as sardines, mackerel and bream are plentiful. Walk along one of the many piers in Trieste and Muggia and you will see small fishing boats with rows of lights attached to them. The lights are used for night-time fishing to attract or stun the fish. You will find mussels, prawns, crabs, cuttlefish and squid in the many small 'pescherie' (fish shops) that dot the streets of Trieste. Most have hand-drawn signs outside to let customers know what has just come in fresh from the night before, and it is common to see people peering through the window of the fish shop to inspect what might become their lunch. Sardines are a favourite with the locals: fried, battered and fried, marinated, stuffed, added to soups or eaten in a sweet-and-sour sauce ('in savor'), a remnant of former Venetian times.

The Bora is the ferocious Alpine wind that blows through the towns on the Adriatic shore from Mount Conero to the Gulf of Trieste. It is strongest in the most northern areas, where it can reach well over 170 kilometres (105 miles) an hour, and is talked about, written about and even sung about in popular culture. It has also influenced the agriculture of the area, as whatever grows must be protected from the Bora or be able to withstand it.

Bianchera, the native olive tree of the area, can withstand the winds, rain and cold, and produce intensely flavoured fruit and olive oil. Fruit and vegetables are similarly challenged by the weather and the rocky terrain of the Carso. Eating seasonally and locally means that in spring you will find bunches of spindly wild asparagus on the market shelves (if you have not gone out and picked them yourself), next to local artichokes and leafy greens such as 'matavilz' (lambs lettuce) and 'radiceto'

(a sweet and small leafy green chicory) used in traditional salads and often served with borlotti beans. In summer there is a small supply of local apricots, figs and plums, the latter used as the filling for traditional potato gnocchi 'con susine' (with plums), and in winter cabbage that is turned into sauerkraut to accompany pork sausages known locally as 'luganighe de cragno'.

Wine is the drink of choice and viticulture has existed here since Roman times. Writing in the first century, Pliny the Elder claimed that Livia, wife of Emperor Augustus and an octogenarian, owed her longevity to wine, specifically to 'pucino' from the hills of the Carso. We don't know whether this refers to what we now call prosecco or to refosco (a robust red grape and wine typical of the Carso). The growing area for the white glera grape that is used to make prosecco has its most easterly and oldest vineyards close to the village of Prosecco, not far from Trieste, and it is clear that the area has produced wine for centuries. Happily and gloriously, it still does. Like their neighbours in the Veneto region, the Triestini love to have a drink, even in the morning; it is not uncommon to hear a local request a 'spritz bianco' (half white wine and half sparkling water, sometimes served on ice) or 'spritz rosso' (half red wine) while you are ordering your coffee at the local bar. You should try it – a spritz bianco can be very refreshing on a hot day, although maybe not first thing in the morning.

Frittata con asparagi selvatici
Wild asparagus omelette

In late spring, if you know where to look and what to look for, you are likely to find wild asparagus growing in the rocky plateau of the Carso, starting from the pre-Alpine hills almost to the Adriatic shore. In the seaside township of Aurisina, where the hill slopes down steeply towards the sea, properties are laden with spindly and bare rows of vines, awakening from the long winter. Tufts of deep green and purple asparagus 'acutifolius' poke out here and there, along fences in pockets that have partial sunlight. Wild asparagus is slightly more bitter than the variety commonly found in shops, and is typically long-stemmed and very thin.

To clean asparagus, you should break or cut off the woody end. It can then be steamed lightly, and dressed with olive oil and a dash of vinegar. Wild asparagus is often paired with eggs, as in this simple omelette, which makes a lovely meal for one. Ideally, it should be accompanied by a glass of dry white wine, such as friulano or malvasia from the Collio, not too far from the Gulf of Trieste. If you can't find wild asparagus, use thin regular asparagus instead.

10–12 wild asparagus spears
(or 4–5 regular spears)

iced water, for refreshing

3 eggs

splash of milk

sea salt and freshly ground
black pepper

small knob of unsalted butter

40 g (1½ oz) Montasio
semi-matured cheese
(or another flavoursome cheese
that melts well), thinly sliced

Wash the asparagus spears and trim the woody ends. Steam for 1–3 minutes until just tender (the cooking time will depend on the size of spears). Refresh in iced water to retain the green colour, then set aside.

Crack the eggs into a bowl, add the milk, salt and pepper and beat until well combined. Set aside.

Heat the butter in a small frying pan over medium heat until just melted (don't let it brown). Pour in the egg mixture, tilting the pan to cover the base evenly, and cook for a couple of minutes until the edges start to cook but the centre is still a bit soft. Layer the cheese on one half of the omelette and place the asparagus spears on top. Using a spatula, fold the other half of the omelette over the filling. Remove from the heat, cover and set aside for a minute or two until the soft centre is cooked and the cheese has melted. Carefully lift from the pan with the spatula and place on a warmed plate. Serve immediately.

SERVES 1

Sarde impanade
Crumbed sardines

Sardines are the most loved fish of the Triestini. The small fishing boats used by traditional fishermen can be seen moored at the 'Molo della Pescheria' (Fishermans wharf) during the day. The boats have rows of lights attached to their frame, which are switched on during night-time fishing to attract or stun fish, and then nets are dropped to catch them. A usual haul includes bream, sea bass, anchovies and sardines. Unlike in southern Italy, where sardines are caught when they are older, larger and have browner flesh, those caught in the northern-most Adriatic waters are under a year old, white-fleshed and around 10 cm (4 inches) in length. Fishermen deliver their catches to the market in the early morning and from there they are distributed to one of the many pescherie that dot the coast of Friuli-Venezia Giulia.

When silvery sardines are really fresh, they are best eaten simply fried or 'impanade' (coated with breadcrumbs and fried until golden). I fillet the fish without a knife by gently separating the head using my fingers and removing the spine and innards all in one. My father taught me how to do this back in our family home, over the laundry sink (so the kitchen sink didn't smell fishy). I try to keep the two fillets of each fish joined in the centre and the tail intact. You can always ask your fishmonger to clean the sardines for you or buy them already filleted.

20 very fresh sardines, ideally about 10 cm (4 in) in length, filleted

50 g (1¾ oz/⅓ cup) plain (all-purpose) flour

1 egg

splash of milk

50 g (1¾ oz/½ cup) dried breadcrumbs, preferably homemade

extra virgin olive oil, for pan-frying

sea salt

lemon wedges, to serve

Wash the filleted sardines and pat them dry with paper towel. Tip the flour into a bowl, whisk together the egg and milk in a second bowl, and pour the breadcrumbs into a third. Dust one fillet at a time in flour (on both sides), dip in the egg wash and then drop into the breadcrumbs, making sure it is well coated. Place each crumbed sardine on a plate.

Pour olive oil into a large shallow frying pan to a depth of 3–5 mm (⅛–¼ in) and heat over medium–high heat. When the oil is hot, carefully add five to seven fillets (depending on the size of your pan) and cook for 1 minute or until the breadcrumbs are golden. Turn them over with tongs and cook the other side for less than a minute. Remove and drain on paper towel. Repeat with the remaining sardines.

Season the sardines with sea salt and serve hot with lemon wedges. If you were in Trieste and it was summer you would probably enjoy them with a cold beer.

SERVES 4 AS AN APPETISER

Sarde in savor alla Triestina
Sardines 'in savor' Trieste style

Another way to enjoy sardines is 'in savor', which allows the small delicate fish to last for several days – even up to a week – once cooked. The Venetians prepare this dish with pine nuts and currants or sultanas, but the Triestina version simply has a bay leaf and onions, or even wild fennel flowers if they are in season.

You will need to start this recipe one day ahead

125 ml (4 fl oz/½ cup) extra virgin olive oil

3 brown onions, thinly sliced on a mandoline

1 fresh or dried bay leaf

125 ml (4 fl oz/½ cup) white wine vinegar

20 fresh sardines, filleted (see recipe introduction, page 264)

plain (all-purpose) flour, for dusting

sea salt

crusty bread, to serve

Heat half the olive oil in a large non-stick frying pan over medium–low heat. Add the onion and bay leaf and cook gently, stirring frequently and adding a bit of water if it starts to brown. After about 20 minutes the onion should be soft and lightly golden. Add the vinegar and cook for another 10 minutes, making sure the onion remains moist (add a bit more water if needed). There should be some liquid left in the pan at the end of cooking. Transfer the onion to a bowl, along with any remaining liquid. Wipe out the pan.

Dust the sardines with flour on both sides. Heat the remaining olive oil in the same pan over medium heat and cook the sardines for about 1 minute each side until pale golden (don't overcook them). Drain on paper towel and season with sea salt.

In a glass or ceramic container, preferably with its own lid, place a thin layer of onion and then a layer of sardines. Repeat the layers three or four times until you have used up all the ingredients, finishing with an onion layer. Press it down with your hands. Drizzle over any remaining onion cooking liquid – there should be enough to keep the sardines quite moist. Cover and place in the fridge for at least 1 day before serving cold with crusty bread.

The sardines will keep in the container in the fridge for up to a week.

SERVES 6–8 AS AN APPETISER

Patate e erbette in tecia
Potato and silverbeet smash

Travel along the Adriatic coast from Trieste to the Istrian peninsula through Slovenia and Croatia and you will find smashed potatoes and greens on menus and kitchen tables. It was a staple of my childhood, one that my mother used to make most weekends, using silverbeet (Swiss chard) picked from my father's garden whenever it was in season. My sister's mother-in-law Lorna came over one day and saw my mother wringing out something dark green over the sink. 'What have you got there, Livia?' she asked. 'Some old socks?' So of course from that day on this mash has been known as 'old socks'.

This simple dish is garlicky, soft and comforting, and is a good match with salt-crusted snapper (see page 200) or barbecued bream (see page 92), although I'm just as happy eating it on its own.

650 g (1 lb 7 oz) potatoes

1 bunch silverbeet (Swiss chard)

2 cloves garlic, finely chopped

2 tablespoons extra virgin olive oil

sea salt and freshly ground black pepper

Wash the potatoes and place in a saucepan of cold water. Cover and bring to the boil, then reduce the heat and cook for about 30 minutes until the potatoes are fork-tender.

Meanwhile, trim the thick stalks from the silverbeet and wash well, then drain and roughly chop. Bring a large saucepan of salted water to the boil. Plunge the silverbeet leaves in the boiling water and cook for a couple of minutes, then drain.

Place the garlic and olive oil in a medium frying pan over medium–low heat. When the garlic becomes fragrant, toss in the silverbeet leaves and cook for a couple of minutes until the leaves are well coated in the garlicky oil. Set aside.

Drain the potatoes and peel, then return them to the pan and roughly mash with a potato masher, making sure you leave a few lumps for texture. Add the silverbeet mixture and stir well to combine.

Season to taste with salt and pepper and serve immediately.

SERVES 6 AS A SIDE DISH

Gnocchetti de pan con burro fuso
Bread gnocchi with butter

Most people associate gnocchi with potato but they can be made with other ingredients, such as ricotta, semolina or even leftover polenta. In the northeast part of Italy, where the food has a strong Austro-Hungarian influence, leftover bread is used to make 'gnocchi di pane' (bread gnocchi), very similar to Austrian 'knödel' or the version eaten in Trentino Alto Adige, 'canederli'. Stale bread is soaked in milk, then squeezed dry and mixed with speck or pancetta, spices and eggs to make large plum-size balls, served in a tasty meat broth.

The Triestini do things a bit differently – their bread gnocchi are always served dry. In her book Ricette Triestine, Istriane e Dalmate (Recipes from Trieste, Istria and Dalmatia) author Iolanda de Vonderweid suggests using a combination of ham, speck and pressed tongue to make gnocchi di pane the size of billiard balls, which are traditionally served with a goulash, ragù or the pan juices from a roast. Mine are a bit smaller, gently poached, rolled in melted butter and dusted with grated parmesan.

500 g (1lb 2 oz) crustless
stale bread, cut into
5 mm (¼ in) cubes

250 ml (8½ fl oz/1 cup) milk

extra virgin olive oil,
for pan-frying

150 g (5½ oz) mixed deli meats
(pancetta, ham, pressed tongue
and/or speck), finely diced

1 large egg, lightly beaten

about 100 g (3½ oz) parmesan,
grated, plus extra to serve

1 tablespoon finely chopped
flat-leaf parsley

sea salt and freshly ground
black pepper

40 g (1½ oz) plain
(all-purpose) flour

100 g (3½ oz) unsalted butter

Place the bread cubes in a medium bowl, pour over the milk and leave to soak for about 15 minutes.

Meanwhile, heat a splash of olive oil in a frying pan over medium heat, add the diced meats and cook for a few minutes.

Remove the bread from the milk and squeeze dry. Place in a large clean bowl, add the cooked meats, egg, parmesan, parsley and salt and pepper to taste. Bring together to make cohesive dough, then cover and rest in the fridge for at least 15 minutes.

Shape the dough into balls the size of a small apricot; if the dough is too wet, add a bit of extra parmesan. Coat the balls lightly in flour and set aside. You should have enough dough to make about 30 balls.

Bring a large saucepan of salted water to the boil. Gently drop in the gnocchi and cook at a slow steady boil for about 10 minutes.

Meanwhile, in a frying pan large enough to fit all the gnocchi, melt the butter over low heat (if your pan isn't large enough, do this in two batches). Remove the gnocchi with a slotted spoon and carefully drop them into the melted butter, tossing to make sure they are well coated.

Serve in warmed bowls generously topped with extra grated parmesan.

SERVES 6

Fusi al Refosco con salsiccia e radicchio
Red fusi with radicchio and pork sausage

'Fusi' are a shape of pasta typical of the northeastern coast of the Adriatic. Squares of egg pasta are wrapped around the handle of a wooden spoon to make an overlapping tube-like shape that looks a bit like penne. A variation of this shape is a triangle of pasta dough rather than a square, with all three points pressed into the centre. Fusi made during the traditional winter slaughter of the pig would be red, tinged with pig's blood, to celebrate the sausages and salumi that had been prepared for the year.

When I was in Trieste researching this book I ate deep-red fusi made with local refosco wine, served with a pork sausage and red radicchio sauce. Dark purple refosco grapes are typical of the Carso and they make a very tannic wine. Refosco is hard to find outside of the area, but merlot makes a respectable substitute. Using red wine in the pasta dough gives a paler (but equally dramatic) colour than the traditional blood red, but it does not impart a lot of flavour. If you don't have the time or inclination to make the pasta just use store-bought penne and enjoy it with the robust pork sausage and radicchio sauce.

1 small head red radicchio

400 g (14 oz) pure
pork sausages

2 tablespoons extra virgin
olive oil

1 large red onion, thinly sliced
on a mandoline, slices halved

125 ml (4 fl oz/½ cup) red wine
(preferably refosco or merlot)

sea salt and freshly ground
black pepper

splash of vincotto or aged
balsamic vinegar

100 g (3½ oz) parmesan, grated

Pasta

600 ml (21 fl oz) red wine
(refosco or merlot)

400 g (14 oz/2⅔ cups)
plain (all-purpose) flour

2 egg yolks

superfine semolina
(semola rimacinata),
for dusting

To make the pasta, pour the wine into a saucepan and place over medium heat. Simmer until it reduces to 200 ml (7 fl oz), then pour into a heatproof jug and set aside to cool.

Follow the instructions on pages 22–23 for making egg pasta, drizzling in the wine as you combine the flour and eggs. Cover and allow to rest for at least 30 minutes.

Dust your work surface with superfine semolina. Cut the pasta dough in half and wrap one half in plastic film while you roll out the other. Using a pasta machine, roll out the dough until it is the desired thickness (I took mine to the third last setting of my machine).

Cut 5–6 cm (2–2½ in) squares of pasta and roll on the diagonal around a wooden dowel (or handle of a wooden spoon) so that opposite points of the squares overlap, then seal the points with your finger dipped in water. The resultant pasta shape will look a bit like hand-formed penne. Dust the prepared shapes with superfine semolina and cover with a clean tea towel to prevent them from drying out while you repeat the process with the remaining pasta.

Break the leaves off the radicchio. Cut out the thick central white spine and shred the leaves finely (about 3 mm/⅛ in wide). Place the shredded leaves in a bowl of water and allow to soak for 15 minutes to remove some of the bitterness. Drain.

Meanwhile, remove the casing from the pork sausages and break the meat into small pieces. Set aside.

Heat the olive oil in a medium frying pan over low heat, add the onion and the drained radicchio and cook for 10–15 minutes until softened. Increase the heat to medium, add the sausage chunks and cook, stirring occasionally, until they are browned all over. Pour in the wine and sauté until the wine starts to evaporate, then reduce the heat and cook for another 5 minutes or until the sauce has thickened. Season to taste with salt and pepper.

Bring a large saucepan of salted water to the boil. Drop in the pasta and cook until al dente (the cooking time will vary, depending on the thickness of the pasta, but it should only take a few minutes). Drain, then add the pasta to the sauce and toss to coat.

Serve on warmed plates, finished with a dash of vincotto or aged balsamic and a generous scattering of parmesan.

SERVES 4

CURED MEATS OF THE CARSO
I SALUMI DEL CARSO

The roads from the Adriatic coast leading inland from Trieste, Muggia and Duino wind steeply inland, cutting through limestone cliff faces and onto the plateau known as the Carso. Tiny towns like Contovello, Prosecco and Santa Croce may be less than a few kilometres (miles) from the coast, but they feel like rural villages, with streets barely wide enough for a car to drive through. The population of these villages is mostly Slovenian, with street signs in two languages (Italian and Slovenian), telling you that the town of Sgonico is also Zgonik, Sales is also Salež, and on it goes. You will hear Slovene spoken just as much as the local Venetian-influenced dialect of Trieste.

CURED MEATS OF THE CARSO

I SALUMI DEL CARSO

The houses that skirt the towns are on small plots of land, each with a vegetable garden growing leafy greens, cabbage and potatoes, a few dozen vines, some olive trees, a couple of chickens laying eggs, a sheep and maybe a pig (or at least a neighbour with a pig) and a legion of languid cats.

The pig has always held an important place in the communities of the Carso. As recounted by Vesna Guštin Grilanc in her book *Xe piu' Giorni che Luganighe* (*There are More Days Than Sausages*), the traditional 'Festa del Maiale' (feast of the pig) was held in winter, any time from November to February. The town butcher would attend the farm and, with the help of family and neighbours, slaughter the animal. It was a day of celebration after a year of tending to the pig; out of respect for the animal, and because of the poverty of the people, none of it would be wasted. The legs, belly, shoulder, cheek, ears, hoofs, and all the innards and blood had a use; the fat or lard was particularly prized, as it would be used as a condiment for the rest of the year. Many parts of the meat were cured into prosciutto, salame, pancetta, capocollo and guanciale, which would feed that family for the entire year, with a portion being set aside to sell in town in order to purchase next year's pig.

Though the Festa del Maiale is not as common in modern times, there is still a thriving industry for pork products on the Carso. My friend Max, born and bred in Trieste and with a keen interest in the traditions of the Carso, took me on a tour of the area, through the narrow streets of Prosecco and Sgonico to an agriturismo called Bajta. 'You will love it here Paola,' he said. 'Wait until you see their prosciutto room.' Bajta is a small farm run by brothers Andrej and Nevo Skerlj and is famous for its prosciutto. We began with a tour of their small shop, a type of butcher shop with pancetta, salami, sausages and various cuts of fresh pork on display behind deli-style windows. On a nearby table, a partially sliced prosciutto sat firmly hugged by a vice, waiting to be sliced thickly by hand, because that's how they serve it around here.

Irena, Andrej's wife, took us through the wine cellars and into a series of darkened underground rooms used for curing meat. As she opened the door to the 'prosciutto room' (as Max called it), a strong smell of salt and deep, heavy earth emerged. Irena turned on the light and the small group of people on the tour let out a collective sigh; there were literally hundreds of prosciutti hanging

on rows of wooden racks on the walls and on the ceiling, adjacent to the rock wall. It was actually a prosciutto cave.

Irena described the pigs they breed at Bajta, a hardy cross between the Duroc and the Large White. They are locally born and bred, fed with local grains and live in the open all year round, free to roam and forage. The hind legs are destined to become prosciutto, a deliciously sweet and moist variety with a good layer of fat around it. To make the prosciutto the hind leg is rubbed with a mixture of garlic, bay leaf, rosemary, salt and 'sugna' (pork fat) and hung for up to 18 months. Bajta produces around 700 of these each year, making it a small producer, but therein lies the beauty of it: a family-run business with a small but true free-range production ensures only the best prosciutto Carsolino.

Max told me that there are even smaller producers than Bajta, not far from the centre of Trieste. 'The only way they can sell their products is at an osmiza,' he said, pointing to a bundle of branches with leaves hung upside-down by the side of the road. We had passed a couple of these bundles at road intersections, sometimes with arrows and signs, other times without. 'That bundle of leaves is called a frasca, and it means there is an osmiza open.' It took me a minute to get my head around it all. The best description is that osmize are temporary informal restaurants in working farms. The frasca is hung out to let you know that you can go and eat there.

To understand their temporary nature, you need to know a bit about the history. Originating from the time that Trieste was ruled by the Austro-Hungarians, osmize were established so that farms could open their doors and sell their products (usually cured meats and sausages, cheeses, eggs and wine) to the public without paying taxes on what they sold. 'Osmiza' comes from the Slovenian word 'osem', which means 'eight' and historically it refers to the number of days that the farm could be open as an osmiza. There are approximately fifty osmize in the province of Trieste, and these days they open for periods of up to a month.

Some osmize have large tiled outdoor dining spaces with lots of tables, and others are small, with only a couple of tables in what looks like a backyard. Inside the farm there is usually a menu board, typically including prosciutto, salami, capocollo, ham served with grated 'kren' (horseradish), hard-boiled eggs, wedges of cheese, bread and jugs of (often young) wine such as white friulano or the rather astringent red refosco.

Meanwhile, larger osmize with a kitchen may sell freshly prepared dishes such as frittata with local herbs or wild asparagus or 'luganega col pan' (pork sausage cooked in bread, served with mustard – and utterly delicious). The food is served on wooden platters and plastic plates; it is very informal and hugely popular. At one osmiza I visited, with a spectacular view of the Gulf of Trieste, there was a group of young patrons strumming guitars and singing between sips of wine and mouthfuls of bread and salami. I couldn't think of a better way to spend a sunny Sunday afternoon.

Back in Trieste on the coast, there are no osmize; instead you'll find buffets, a curious word for a café-style restaurant that serves mainly pork. They are similarly informal, and were typically frequented by early-morning waterfront workers, who would buy snacks (called a 'ribechin' in the local dialect) standing up at the bar. One of the most famous, Buffet da Pepi, is more than a hundred years old, and its menu celebrates every part of the pig. A typical dish is a platter of sliced sausages (wurstel and cragno), cotechino, tongue, ear, belly and other parts, boiled and served with grated horseradish and mustard. You will often find legs of ham baked in a bread crust (prosciutto in crosta di pane). The ham is then sliced thickly by hand, encased in freshly baked bread and eaten with mustard – all very hearty and very Austrian. In fact, the typical accompaniment to platters of pork is a side of sauerkraut and a stein of local tap beer. It almost feels like you are in Vienna rather than Italy, except the voices around you are speaking that particular lilting Venetian dialect.

Sugo di gallina
Chicken sugo

Plump breasts and meaty thighs are what we have come to expect when we eat chicken, but there is much to be said for cooking with an older chook – the ones sometimes called broilers, which have passed their egg-laying prime and are lean and flavoursome from running around the barnyard. I would buy this type of chicken from the Slovenian butcher at the market in Trieste. He'd bring the chickens down from the Carso, and sell them whole or halved, chopped into pieces if you like. They only had a small amount of meat but it was deliciously tender when cooked at length, the skin and bones packing a tasty punch in a broth or a sugo.

Sugo di gallina does not traditionally have a lot of meat in it, and what is there is so tender it's barely hanging onto the bone. If you can't find a lean broiler chicken, use a combination of chicken thighs and drumsticks, bones intact. If you do this you may need to reduce the cooking time by 20–30 minutes so the meat does not dry out. This is best served with your favourite pasta or gnocchi, finished with a good sprinkling of parmesan.

1½ tablespoons extra virgin olive oil

1 large brown onion, finely chopped

2 cloves garlic, crushed

1.2 kg (2 lb 10 oz) chicken (preferably a whole broiler), washed, patted dry and cut into 12 pieces

2 teaspoons sweet paprika

½-1 teaspoon freshly ground black pepper

sea salt

2 small rosemary sprigs

125 ml (4 fl oz/½ cup) dry white wine

2 tablespoons tomato paste

80 ml (2½ fl oz/⅓ cup) boiling water

grated parmesan, to serve

Heat the olive oil in a large saucepan over low heat, add the onion and cook, stirring occasionally, for 20–30 minutes until soft and starting to fall apart (don't let it brown), then add the garlic and cook until fragrant.

Meanwhile, place the chicken pieces in a bowl and toss with the paprika, pepper and about 1 teaspoon of salt. Rub the spices into the chicken pieces.

Add the chicken pieces to the onion mixture, increase the heat to medium and cook for a few minutes until browned. Flip them over and cook for a few more minutes until nicely browned all over. Add the rosemary and half the wine and continue to cook, stirring occasionally, until the wine has evaporated. Add the remaining wine and cook for another 10 minutes or until the wine has evaporated again.

Dissolve the tomato paste in the boiling water, add to the pan and stir to combine. Cover and simmer for 1½ hours (or 1 hour if you are using thighs and drumsticks), stirring regularly. The chicken should release quite a bit of liquid, especially if you are using thighs and drumsticks, but feel free to add a bit more water if it looks dry. Taste the sauce and add salt if needed.

The sugo is ready when the meat is tender and falling off the bones. Remove any smaller bones from the chicken pieces (especially if you are using a chopped whole chicken), then serve topped with grated parmesan.

SERVES 4–6

Canocchie alla busara
Shrimps in a busara sauce

The locals call them 'canoce', a curious-looking crustacean with a shell that has what looks like a pair of eyes on its tail. They are, in fact, squilla mantis shrimp ('canocchie' in Italian), and are common in the Adriatic Sea. Fresh canocchie will look plump and feel soft, and the shell will release a briny liquid when cut, adding flavour to the sauce in which they are cooked.

Busara sauce is typical of the Adriatic coast north of Venice, the 'busara' probably being the pan that fisherman used on their boats to cook it. Traditionally made with white wine, I like to add seedless tomato pulp, creating a rich sauce in which to briefly cook the shrimp. The whole lot is mopped up with bread, though soft polenta or pasta would also be delicious.

If you can't find squilla mantis shrimp, scampi would make a worthy substitute – both have sweet delicately flavoured flesh, although scampi are firmer.

16–20 squilla mantis shrimp or scampi

1½ tablespoons extra virgin olive oil

1 small brown onion, finely diced

1 clove garlic, peeled, left whole and lightly crushed

125 ml (4 fl oz/½ cup) dry white wine

1 x 400 g (14 oz) tin tomato pulp or chopped tomatoes (without seeds)

sea salt and freshly ground black pepper

chopped flat-leaf parsley, to garnish

crusty bread, to serve

The squilla mantis shrimp has a flat underside and little shell fins to help it swim, a rounded upper side (the same side as the pretend 'eyes' are located) and sides with sharp edges. To prepare the shrimp, start by washing them and patting them dry. Use kitchen scissors to cut off the legs along the body, as well as the softer little fins on the underside. Make sure this area is clean as it can accumulate sand or dirt (rinse under running water if needed). I also remove part of the head, just the tip with the antennae and the eyes, then the other set of legs (or arms) just below the head. Leaving the rest of the head and claws intact will impart greater flavour to the sauce (and the claws contain small amount of meat as well) but some people prefer to remove all the head and the claws. It's up to you.

Using the point of a sharp knife, make an incision through the shell starting just above the tail on the upper side and moving towards the head. Some water should come out (this is good as it means that it's fresh). Making this incision will make the flesh easier to remove when eating. Keep the crustacean on its flat surface so you don't lose any of the flavoursome liquid in the body. If there is an obvious digestive track you can remove it, though I usually leave it in place.

Heat the olive oil in a large frying pan over low heat, add the onion and cook for 5 minutes or until lightly coloured, then add the crushed garlic clove and cook for a minute until fragrant. Add the shrimps, belly-side down, in a single layer if possible. Cover and cook for a few minutes or until the shrimps are less transparent and have taken on a pinkish hue. Remove them with tongs and set aside. The shrimps should have released some of their juices and these will make a base for the sauce.

Increase the heat to medium–high and add the wine. Let it bubble away and evaporate for a few minutes, then add the tomato. Reduce the heat to low and simmer, covered, for 15 minutes, adding water if starts looking dry. Season well. Return the shrimps to the pan and cook for a few minutes until they are warmed through. Finish with a good grinding of black pepper and a scattering of parsley and serve with crusty bread to mop up the juices.

SERVES 4

Gulasch alla Triestina
Beef goulash Trieste style

Goulash doesn't sound Italian at all; in fact, its origins are in Hungary. In the book Trieste, la Tradizione a Tavola *(Trieste, Tradition at the Table) by the Accademia Italiana della Cucina, there is a whole chapter on goulash in Trieste. It describes how every good cook has a recipe that was handed down through the generations from when Trieste was part of the Austro-Hungarian Empire. It has become part of the local culture and winter wouldn't be the same without goulash on traditional tables.*

I follow a few simple rules: onion and beef should be in equal proportions, and the meat should be muscular, not too lean. Trieste-style goulash is traditionally made with lard (although these days most people use olive oil) and the onions are cooked long and slow until they become a sticky sweet paste, before adding beef and paprika. With a side of mashed potatoes or potato gnocchi, it makes for a hearty winter meal.

100 ml (3½ fl oz) extra virgin olive oil

700 g (1 lb 9 oz) brown onions, thinly sliced on a mandoline

700 g (1 lb 9 oz) chuck steak, cut into 1 cm (½ in) cubes

80 ml (2½ fl oz/⅓ cup) red wine

2 teaspoons smoked paprika

2 teaspoons sweet paprika

2 fresh or dried bay leaves

1 rosemary sprig

1 tablespoon tomato paste,

300 ml (10½ fl oz) hot beef stock or water

sea salt and freshly ground black pepper

Heat 70 ml (2¼ fl oz) of the olive oil in a large heavy-based saucepan over low heat, add the onion and cook, stirring regularly, for 30 minutes or until the onion is very soft and translucent (don't let it brown).

Meanwhile, heat the remaining olive oil in a large frying pan over medium–high, drop in the meat and sear on all sides for a few minutes until it is nicely browned. Remove the meat and deglaze the pan with the wine, scraping any bits caught on the base of the pan and allowing some of the liquid to evaporate. Pour the wine into the pan with the cooked onion, and add the beef.

Stir in the smoked and sweet paprika, bay leaves and rosemary sprig. Dissolve the tomato paste in the hot stock or water and add to the pan. Season to taste with salt and pepper, then cover and simmer over low heat for about 1½ hours until the beef is tender. Add a splash of water if it starts to dry out. Taste and adjust the seasoning if needed, then serve.

SERVES 6

Strudel di mele di Livia
Livia's apple strudel

Whenever I am in Trieste I eat quite a bit of apple strudel as I am on the lookout for one to rival my mother's. Mostly I am disappointed, as they invariably have flaky buttery pastry and large chunks of apple – they are very nice but not like mamma's. She tells me that she got the recipe from the Italian social club she used to frequent with ladies from my father's home town. 'Strudel di mele' was made for special occasions, and she always made two: the first one would be polished off the same day (my father had a very sweet tooth), and the second one would last a few days, although not many as it was hard to have just one slice.

The pastry is made with olive oil and is stretched very thin, initially with a rolling pin and then with your hands, to the point where you could read the newspaper (or a love letter) through it. The filling contains grated apple, lemon zest, cocoa, pine nuts and grappa-soaked sultanas, the latter from a jar in the fridge that is constantly replenished.

This strudel is best eaten cold, several hours after it is made when the pastry has softened and wrapped itself around the silky apple purée. It is even better the next day.

1 small egg yolk

splash of milk

caster (superfine) sugar,
for sprinkling (optional)

Pastry

2 teaspoons caster
(superfine) sugar

220 g (7¾ oz) plain
(all-purpose) flour

2½ tablespoons mild-tasting
olive oil

Filling

7 large tart apples
(such granny smith)

50 g (1¾ oz) unsalted butter

3 heaped tablespoons dried
breadcrumbs

2–3 tablespoons granulated
sugar (depending on how tart
your apples are)

1 scant tablespoon pine nuts

1 scant tablespoon unsweetened
dark cocoa powder

finely grated zest of 1 lemon

3 tablespoons sultanas (golden
raisins), soaked in grappa or
brandy for at least an hour

To make the pastry, place the sugar and 180 g (6½ oz) of the flour in a bowl and make a well in the centre. Pour the olive oil and 125 ml (4 fl oz/½ cup) of water into the well and stir with a wooden spoon until well combined. Place half the remaining flour on your work surface and tip the pastry onto the flour. Knead for about 10 minutes or the dough is smooth but has a stretch to it (like a loose pasta dough), adding more flour if it gets too sticky. It's fine if you have some flour left over (you will need it later). Wrap the dough in plastic film and let it rest at room temperature for 30 minutes.

Preheat the oven to 180°C (350°F). Line a large baking tray with baking paper.

To make the filling, peel, core and coarsely grate the apples into a large bowl. Melt the butter in a small saucepan over low heat, add the breadcrumbs and mix well, then remove from the heat and set aside. You will finish the filling after you've rolled out the dough.

Dust your work surface with the remaining flour. Remove the pastry from the plastic film and knead for a few minutes, incorporating a bit of the flour from your work surface as you go. Start rolling out the pastry with a rolling pin, flipping it over every minute or so as you stretch it out. It should be around 50 cm x 40 cm (20 in x 16 in) by now, or thereabouts. Carefully lift the sheet of dough onto a large clean tea towel. Now do the final stretching by hand, by carefully placing your hands under the pastry sheet and gently stretching any sections that are thicker. It should now be about 55 cm x 45 cm (22 in x 18 in). If it is smaller than this, you have not stretched it thinly enough (as I mentioned earlier, it should be thin enough for you to read through). When you are ready to assemble the strudel, turn the pastry so the longer edge is closest to you.

Lightly squeeze and drain the grated apples (drink the lovely apple juice that is left behind). Scatter the apple over the pastry, leaving a 4 cm (1½ in) gap on the two shorter sides, and a 12 cm (4¾ in) gap on the edge of pastry closest to you. The apple filling should go quite close to the pastry edge furthest from you. Scatter the buttery breadcrumbs, sugar, pine nuts, cocoa, lemon zest and drained sultanas evenly over the apple.

Starting from the long edge furthest from you, use the tea towel to help you roll the strudel towards you into a long sausage enclosing the filling – don't roll it too tightly. It will finish up on the strip of pastry without any filling on it. Fold down the two ends of the sausage and carefully lift it onto the prepared tray, curving it into a horse-shoe shape. Whisk together the egg yolk and milk, and brush over the top of the strudel. Scatter on a bit of sugar if you like.

Bake for 15 minutes, then reduce the temperature to 170°C (340°F) and cook for a further 50–55 minutes. About 15 minutes before it's ready, check that the strudel is not browning too much and lower the temperature to 160°C (315°F) if necessary. It should be a deep golden colour.

Let it cool to room temperature before serving; in fact, it's actually better the next day. The strudel will keep in an airtight container in the fridge for 5 days or so.

SERVES 10–12

PESCHERIA

FUORI MENU
- MINESTRA DE BOBICI   € 8,00
- JOTA   € 8,00
- TAGLIATELLE c/TARTUFO   € 9,50

- PASTA c/GOULAS   € 8,00

- GNOCCHI NERI c/SALMONE   € 13,00

- GNOCCHI c/GAMBERI   € 10,00
        E UN BUON
   BICCHIERE DI VINO

PANINI:
CRUDO   GUANCIALE   SALAME
PANCETTA   MORTADELLA
                PORCHETTA

Peri petorai
Baby pears cooked in spiced wine

Italians have a fear of catching cold. When I was growing up I was frequently instructed to tuck in my singlet or cover my neck or close the door to avoid getting a 'giro d'aria' (hit of air) and catching a cold. My mother gave me freshly squeezed orange juice every morning during my school years, in part to protect me from such an eventuality.

And so we come to the story of 'peri petorai', warm spicy pears that are meant to ward off respiratory illnesses caused by the Alpine Bora wind that blows through the Gulf of Trieste. In days gone by 'el petoraler' would stand on the streets selling the small volpine (foxy) pears cooked in syrupy red wine to late-night shoppers and theatre patrons, and they would eat them knowing they were well protected from the icy winds.

I follow Mady Fast's recipe from her book Mangiare Triestino (Eat Trieste) *to make petorai, using cloves as well as cinnamon. If you can't find volpine pears, just use the smallest pears you can find. In Australia small corella pears work well.*

750 ml (25½ fl oz/3 cups) red wine (preferably refosco or merlot)

150 g (5½ oz) caster (superfine) sugar

1 cinnamon stick (or 2 teaspoons ground cinnamon)

3 cloves

peel of 1 orange, in strips

12 small pears (or 4 larger ones)

mascarpone or vanilla ice cream, to serve (optional)

Preheat the oven to 180°C (350°F).

Place the wine, sugar, cinnamon, cloves and orange peel in a saucepan and warm over medium heat until the sugar has dissolved. Remove from the heat and set aside.

Carefully peel the pears and place them upright in a baking dish, trimming a bit off the base to make them sit better if needed. Ideally you want the pears to fit quite snugly. Pour the wine mixture over the pears to cover and bake for 15 minutes for small pears, or 20 minutes or more for larger pears. Check that the pears are tender by inserting a thin skewer – it should go in without any resistance. Using tongs, carefully remove the pears from the dish and set aside.

Strain the liquid, discarding the peel and spices. Pour it back into the pan and simmer over medium–high heat until reduced to a thick syrup.

Serve the warm pears and syrup just as they are, or with a spoonful of mascarpone or vanilla ice cream.

SERVES 4

Presnitz
Fruit and nut spiral cake from Trieste

Is it a gubana, presnitz or putizza? These three typical cakes of Friuli-Venezia Giulia have a lot of similarities: essentially their fillings (nuts, dried fruit and a good splash of alcohol) and their shape (more or less a spiral). The differences relate to their town of origin and the type of pastry used, and getting them mixed up is a dead giveaway that you're not a local.

Presnitz is said to have been a variation on a putizza and was first made in honour of the visit of Sissi (beloved Empress of Austria and Queen of Hungary) to Trieste in 1856. Buttery puff pastry surrounds a filling of boozy sultanas, ground nuts, chocolate, honey and orange zest. It is the only cake of the three that doesn't have yeast so it looks smaller than the others. The filling tastes very good on its own and I have been known to eat a good many spoonfuls while preparing it (just to check the flavours are balanced, obviously). My spiral is a bit more tightly wound up than you usually find in Trieste, which is just the way I like it.

If you are making your own pastry you will need to start this recipe at least four hours ahead so it has sufficient time to rest. If you're not making the pastry yourself (and this is fine – it is quite labour intensive), use a 375 g (13 oz) packet of good-quality store-bought puff pastry to make the cakes.

160 g (5¾ oz/1 cup) sultanas (golden raisins), soaked in 2½ tablespoons white rum for at least 2 hours

3 tablespoons pine nuts, ground

160 g (5¾ oz) hazelnuts, toasted and ground

100 g (3½ oz) walnuts, ground

3 tablespoons almonds, toasted and ground

50 g (1¾ oz) sweet plain biscuits, crushed

40 g (1½ oz) caster (superfine) sugar

70 g (2½ oz) dark chocolate (45% cocoa solids), grated

2 tablespoons honey

finely grated zest of 1 orange

⅛ teaspoon salt

2 eggs, separated

splash of milk

Puff pastry

175 g (6 oz) plain (all-purpose) flour

⅛ teaspoon salt

up to 80 ml (2½ fl oz/⅓ cup) chilled water

125 g (4½ oz) chilled unsalted butter

To make the pastry, place 125 g (4½ oz) of flour in a mound on a work surface; add the salt and then make a well in the centre. Pour about 1 tablespoon of water into the well, working it into the flour using the tines of a fork. When you have worked it in, add a bit more water and work that in. Keep adding small amounts of water and working it in until the dough starts to come together. How much water you will need depends on the humidity in the air, so the amount will vary according to when and where you make the dough. It should have the consistency of a loose pasta dough. Form it into a ball, wrap it in plastic film and let it rest in the fridge for 30 minutes.

Place about 25 g (1 oz) of flour on your work surface (a cool surface such as stone or marble is best), then put the whole piece of butter on the flour. Working quickly so it doesn't start to soften and melt, dust the butter in the flour and then roll it out with your rolling pin slightly, trying to incorporate some of the flour. Flip it over and repeat – you are trying to incorporate as much of the flour as possible. Roll the butter into a rectangle approximately 18 cm x 5 cm (7¼ in x 2 in). If the butter starts to melt or soften too much, wrap it in plastic film and put it in the fridge for 10 minutes before continuing. By now the dough should have rested for long enough.

Roll out the dough on your floured work surface to a 20 cm x 8 cm (8 in x 3¼ in) rectangle. Place the block of butter on top, dust with a bit more flour and roll lengthways. Now fold it over like a letter by folding the top third into the middle and the bottom third over that. Rotate the pastry a quarter turn and repeat, rolling it into a longish rectangle, then folding it like a letter. Repeat once more, then wrap the pastry in plastic film and let it rest in the fridge for 30 minutes.

Repeat the process of rolling, folding and turning the dough, then resting it in the fridge four more times, remembering to dust with extra flour if the pastry becomes sticky at any point.

Start making the filling when you have completed the first rolling, folding and resting of the dough (or about 2 hours ahead if you are using store-bought pastry). Place the drained sultanas, ground nuts, crushed biscuits, sugar, chocolate, honey, orange zest, salt and egg whites in a large bowl and mix well. You should have a thick but spreadable delicious-smelling filling. Cover the bowl and rest in the fridge for 2 hours.

Preheat the oven to 180°C (350°F). Line a large baking tray with baking paper.

Roll out your pastry on a lightly floured surface until it measures about 50 cm x 25 cm (20 in x 10 in). Cut it in half lengthways so you have two long strips of pastry. Divide the filling in half. Place one long compact log of filling along the length of one pastry strip, leaving a gap of about 4 cm (1½ in) at each end. Carefully roll up the pastry to completely enclose the filling and fold down the two ends. Coil the log into a loose spiral and carefully lift it onto the prepared tray. Repeat with the remaining pastry strip and filling.

Whisk together the egg yolks and milk, then brush the egg wash generously over the two presnitzs. Bake for 35–40 minutes until golden and the pastry is cooked through.

Allow to cool completely, then cut into slices with a serrated knife to serve. The presnitzs will keep in an airtight container in the fridge for up to 3 days.

MAKES 2 SMALL CAKES

Ringraziamenti
Thank you

This book is dedicated to my aunts and uncles in Italy: Livio, Dina, Mario, Clara and Vincenzina, some of whom are no longer with us. These special people hosted me, loved me and shared meals with me during my many trips back to my homeland on the coast of the Adriatic Sea.

Special thanks to my mother Livia for being the constant inspiration on my food journey, my husband Mark for being my companion during my research trip and being by my side through the cooking, photographing, writing and editing of *Adriatico* and my daughter Tamara for her enthusiasm, laughter and love. Special thanks to Verdiana who tirelessly helped me in the kitchen, and to Ian for the photos of the Venetian Lagoon he generously gave me.

Thanks to those who inspired my recipes and made my journey along the coast that much easier: Max Miliç, Ksenija and Tomiza Šperanda, Enrica Bienna, Domenica Settembre, Joe Caputo, Francesco de Padova, Maria Antonietta di Viesti, Gianni di Biase, Lazzaro Russo, Giovanni from the Oasi degli Agrumi, Giulia Scappaticcio, Emiliana dell'Arciprete, Fausto di Nella, Maura Amoroso, Matilde Bracciale, Matteo del Nobile, Rosa from the Fabbrica del Bocconotto, Marco and Luca Caldora, Monica Sirotti, Sandro Rocchetti, Letizia Magnani, Elisa and Davide from the Parco della Salina di Cervia, Gabriella Zuliani, Lucilla Marcellino, Matteo Bisol, Enrica Rocca, Irene Skerlj and Alice Adams.

Thanks to my recipe testers for their enthusiasm and helpful feedback: Vanessa Miles, Carmen Pricone, Nichola Midgely, Linda Castrilli, Corinne Blackett, Giulia Porro, Irene Mavrogiannis, Paula Hagiefremidis, Jessica Fransson, Olivia Windsor, Eti Antonova-Baumann, Vanessa Baca, Sue Kirkland, Rosemarie Scavo, Cristina Pepe, Tyana Viti, Max Halley, Katrina Alviano and Emma Torcasio.

Thank you to all my followers on *Italy on my mind* and on Instagram for your comments, encouragement and engagement with my posts. I wouldn't be here without you all.

And finally, many thanks to Paul McNally at Smith Street Books for giving me a second opportunity at writing a cookbook and the creative freedom to take it where I wanted; Rachel Carter who took the time to read my entire blog before expertly editing my recipes; Michelle Mackintosh for the beautiful design and the cover which is better than I ever imagined it could be; Heather Menzies and Andy Warren for the layout and image tweaks, and to Lucy Heaver for patiently and skillfully bringing it all together to make it the book you now have in your hands.

A proposito di me
About me

Paola Bacchia was born in Melbourne, Australia. Her parents were born in the northeast corner of Italy and migrated to Australia in the aftermath of World War II. They built a home with the kitchen and garden at its heart.

Paola remembers her papà coming in from the backyard, his arms filled with freshly picked tomatoes and zucchini, and her mamma pounding the basil to make fragrant pestos to be stirred through pasta. Fresh, simple, seasonal and made from scratch. These are the things that are important to Paola in her approach to food.

Paola is a dentist by profession, but a few years ago she realised she would rather be making pasta than drilling molars, so she started writing Italy on my mind – an award-winning blog that shares family recipes and food memories. She learned photography along the way and established a cooking school in her home in Melbourne.

Paola has run several residential cooking workshops at the Anna Tasca Lanza Cooking School in Sicily, along with photography and styling workshops, and leads food and wine tours in Trieste and other Italian locations. She wrote, photographed and styled her first cookbook, *Italian Street Food*, published by Smith Street Books. She cooks regularly with her mother, from whom she continues to draw inspiration, and travels to Italy each year to spend time with family and learn more more about Italian food and wine culture.

Paola regularly posts stories, recipes and photos on her website www.italyonmymind.com.au and photos on Instagram @italyonmymind

Adriatico is Paola's second book.

Indice
INDEX

Published in 2018 by Smith Street Books
Collingwood | Melbourne | Australia
smithstreetbooks.com

ISBN: 978-1-925418-72-9

CIP data is available from the National Library of Australia

Publisher: Paul McNally
Editor: Rachel Carter
Project editor: Lucy Heaver, Tusk studio
Cover designer: Michelle Mackintosh
Design concept: Michelle Mackintosh
Design layout: Heather Menzies, Studio 31 Graphics
Photographer: Paola Bacchia
Stylist: Paola Bacchia

Printed & bound in China by C&C Offset Printing Co., Ltd.

Book 64
10 9 8 7 6 5 4 3 2 1